I Am

A collection of inspiring short stories for teenage girls.

I Am

Ashleigh Morgan

I Am
A collection of inspiring short stories for teenage girls.

Published by:
Ashleigh Morgan

ISBN: 978-0615938585

Table of Contents

I Am Beautiful

I had to face the fact that my life sucked. Years of moving had finally caught up with my emotions. It seemed that every other month my family had to move around the country. Currently, six moves later, we were moving to New Jersey to live on my Aunt Valerie's rental property. After all, having bought and sold six houses, my parents were losing hope that we could keep any of our homes. Of course it was only natural that we were losing money. My life didn't just suck; it was over from the first time that we moved.

When Dad first broke the news to me, I just blew up. I guess he thought dinner time was the best time to tell my sisters Jade, Jocelyn, and me.

"Why are you doing this to us again?" I screamed from across the table.

"It's not personal," he snapped.

"Sure feels personal," I said, pushing the mashed potatoes around on my plate.

"I could say the same about your imprudent hair extensions."

There he was again trying to sound overly educated with big words. What he was really saying was that my hair looked outrageous and disgraceful and that I humiliated him with my appearance. I heard that a million times from him before and decided to ignore the comment once again.

"I'm just saying, this is the fourth time…just this year!"

Jocelyn, who is seventeen, muttered, "And it's only October."

Mom wouldn't look away from my two year old sister, Jade, while trying to get her to eat. Jade kept shaking her head in protest.

I blurted, "I just don't understand why-"

"It's done," Dad said.

I pushed my plate away without having taken a bite and jumped up. "I don't know why I ever bother to unpack. Next time you make a promise, why don't you keep it?" I ran out of the kitchen and upstairs to my room, making sure I stomped each step in protest. By the time I reached my room, tears were rolling down my cheeks. I ran over and fell onto my bed, taking the bumble bee pillow pet Dad had given me when I was little and threw it at the door. Then I spotted the picture of Katelyn on my dresser. She was my best friend from our third move. I jumped up and walked over, slamming the photo face down.

* * *

Six days later, I turned my bedroom light off and took all of my boxes downstairs to the moving trucks. Mom and Dad were loading our car with all of our carry-on bags, while a bald man in a U-Haul truck piled all of our possessions onto three trucks.

"I hope you're happy 'Mr. and Mrs. we aren't moving again'!" I said as I passed my parents.

"Jasleen, watch your mouth," Mom said.

"Whatever!" I went back inside and turned off all of the lights in the kitchen. It was becoming the same routine. I took one last look at house number six. I really thought that this house was the last one we would have to move into. It was certainly the prettiest house in the whole neighborhood. Oh, well.

Jocelyn and Jade were already in the car. Jocelyn's head was resting on the car window, her eyes staring out at nothing. She mumbled, "So, on to house number seven. You ready?"

I sighed at the very idea, even though I knew that a new school would give me another fresh start.

"Jo," Mom yelled, "go get Jade a snack before we leave!"

"Okay!" Jocelyn yelled back. "Come on, Jade. Let's get you a snack."

"Yay!" Jade shouted as Jocelyn unbuckled her seat belt.

"What would you like, Jay?"

"Pwetzels."

Jocelyn got out of the car with Jade.

When they were gone, I started to think about the fresh start I would be getting all over again. I wouldn't be a "slime ball" or a "freak show" anymore. I wouldn't have to hear the cheerleaders chant, "Two- four- six- eight! Who's the girl we really hate? Jasleen! The freak! Yeah!" or "Two- four- six- eight! Who needs to move out of our way? Jasleen! The freak! Yeah!"

I swear if I had to hear that cheer one more time, someone was going to the hospital with a black eye! I had been bullied in all of my schools. I tried being the real me, nice. Unfortunately, everyone thought that because I was kind, I was weak. So, within the last two moves, I decided to put on a tough act, and it worked! I now knew how I would survive New Jersey. It wouldn't be hard. I'm a great actress, believe or not.

"That's it! That's the last of it." Mom announced, getting into the car. Jocelyn and Jade got back in with Jade sitting between us in her car seat. I helped buckle her in.

Dad climbed in to the driver's seat. He glanced into the rearview mirror. "Jasleen, I know this is a little random, but why are you wearing those disastrous purple extensions again?"

"Because I can! Why can't you just deal with me, the way I am?" I growled. If I had a dime for every time I had to ask that question…

"My God, girl!" He sighed.

"Maybe it's because I'm not pretty like Jo!" At least he didn't think so.

Jocelyn put her hand on my shoulder. "You are beautiful," she whispered.

"Shut up, Jo!" I yelled. If I had a penny for every time she said that.

"Jasleen, honey, you are beautiful. You really are!" Mom tried.

"Well that's one word for it," Dad mumbled.

"Ben, chill!" Mom shouted. "Tell your daughter that you believe in her. She is fine the way she is."

"Jasleen…. You…. You, you are… beautiful… just the way you are." He gave me a fake smile. "Are you happy now, Joanna?"

"You might not like me. You're right. I might be ugly in your eyes! But at least I know to think about my family before moving all around the world!"

Mom was crying, which made Jade start to cry. For the rest of the trip in the car and on the plane, no one talked. Not even Jade, who normally did not shut up.

Our new house sat on the corner, between the Carols and the Kirkwood families, according to the names plastered on their mailboxes. I wondered what they were like. Were they like the Johnsons- creepy and old, or like the Ramonas- the hippie family? You have no idea how many times I wanted to tell them where to put their magic rainbows. Maybe these neighbors had a cute little boy like the Murphy's. Or maybe they smelled bad like the Wilson family. I can guarantee you that they all did not realize how good they had it to be able to stay in one house.

After starting to unpack, my mom told Jocelyn and me about our new high school. The next morning, we met all of our teachers and received copies of our schedules. It was the Friday before the fifth week of school began, and in that weekend I looked around at all of the middle class homes in New Jersey. These people were not filthy rich, but they were pretty wealthy. Good, at least I wouldn't be dealing with stuck up snobs like Kelsey Danowitz from move number three…

* * *

"Class, please take your seats," Mrs. Regan, a tall bronzed woman, with pink rimmed glasses, said. "We have a new student, all the way from sunny California!"

I didn't have a seat, yet, so I just stood at the front of the classroom, letting Mrs. Regan begin her introduction.

"This is Jasleen Tyler. Class, let's make her feel welcomed!" The whole class clapped, but I didn't look up. I didn't want any new friends, and they certainly did not make me feel welcomed with their piercing stares. Even if I did meet a friend, what was the point anyway? I knew the new drill, by heart: you go to a new school, meet new friends, tried to fit in, got bullied, then you moved away. That's the way life was, to me at least.

Dad was a doctor in the military. He was constantly being relocated across the country. So far, Texas, Idaho, Michigan, Alaska (who knows why?), Maine, and California were my homelands. There was really no point of making friends and then leaving them over and over again. I felt lonely, but I didn't like hurting them. Wouldn't you be hurt if your best friend moved all around America? Besides it wasn't like everyone was begging to be my friend. I wasn't exactly the prettiest girl on the block. If you wanted to be my friend, you were either desperate or on drugs. If you saw my solid body with glasses, thunder thighs, and extra-frizzy long hair, wouldn't you freak out too?

As a way to be accepted, I decided to be a lot of different things. I tried to be a mean girl, then a brainiac, a punk rocker chic, a girly girl, and a skater. The only one that seemed to work was dressing in the punk style. I caked on my dark eye shadows and mascara, and I changed my hair adding different colored streaks. I only wore black and dark purple things, like plaid skirts and black jackets. My definition of beautiful was trying to be in with the latest punk trends. I wasn't hurting anyone, so who cared what I wore?

I was never naturally beautiful like Jo. Her hair was perfect with natural loose curls. She didn't wear glasses, and she had perfect skin, a perfect smile, and a perfect figure. She had been a model, since she was twelve, and up until now has modeled for Guess, Hollister, Pantene, and Seventeen. She was the youngest model I've ever heard of to be so successful. Naturally, she was a boy magnet. During her freshman year, a senior guy asked her out. A senior! Jo was untouchable. Last year, her junior year, she gave an impressive speech about the degrading thoughts of teenagers at the senior graduation. She even got the attention of Oprah. In one word, she was amazing, and I've always wanted to be her.

"Jasleen!"

I snapped back to reality. "What?"

"Casey asked where you have lived," Mrs. Regan said.

I looked over at a short girl with straight gold hair, and decided to start my act "Well, Casey, you seem like a decent girl, so I'll answer your question. I have moved six times, but naming the locations would be just as boring as listening to this teacher speak!" The whole class cracked up.

"Ms. Tyler, that kind of disrespect will not be tolerated in my classroom!"

"Then, can I say it", I made air quotes, "*outside* of your class room?" I asked with a sneaky grin.

The class started gossiping.

"Where did she come from?" one boy asked, pointing at my hair.

"No one was dumb enough to tell Mrs. Regan off before." another girl said.

I frowned. They were supposed to laugh! *NOT* gossip!

"Oh, class!" Mrs. Regan yelled. "Settle down, now!" She turned my way. "Take your seat," she snapped, pointing to an empty desk.

"Well-," I started.

"Now!"

It wasn't like me to have an outburst. I didn't want to be this way, but I had to be tough and show that I was capable of handling some dumb teacher. From the looks on the students' faces, I was doing a pretty good job. I walked to the desk and sat down.

"Class, now that comedy hour is over, let's begin." She clapped twice, and I guess that was a signal, because everyone froze and faced forward. "Class, you remember Ms. Jones, right?"

Everyone sighed and moaned.

"Relax! She doesn't have another community service project in mind."

The class cheered. "This year she is having a fundraising fashion show for all of you who wish to look... how do they say it today?" she mumbled. "Ah...bling! bling!" The class moaned again. "Relax! You should be happy you aren't writing an essay right now." She sighed. "Anyway, Riley, I mean Ms. Jones asked me to do her a favor and mention it to you. Any volunteers?"

"Of course you know I'll win, so buy tickets!" said a rich looking preppy girl. She stood up and curtseyed.

"Anastasia, please sit!" Mrs. Regan said.

Anastasia curtseyed again before taking a seat. She was wearing a violet low cut Juicy Couture t-shirt, and black yoga pants with black Uggs that had the initials, A K embroidered in them. I wanted to tell her to put some real clothes on. She had her light brown hair up in a high ponytail, and she was wearing a silver tiara, also customized with diamonds and those initials. She looked like a spoiled little brat, and I was almost positive that she was not a real princess. Only a stuck up girl would ever think to wear a tiara just because.

"Well," Anastasia continued, as though making sure I knew how important she thought she was. "We all know that I have won six pageants and have been in numerous magazines and commercials, so don't expect to win!"

"Turn to page 119 and begin exercise C," Mrs. Regan said impatiently.

"That book is organized so that all of the exercises are in the back," a girl across from me whispered.

"Thanks," I said, rolling my eyes.

When a boy across the aisle glanced over at me, I said, "Stay out of my way! That shirt is almost as hideous as those shoes!" He flushed to a deep red and turned towards the front of the classroom.

"Geez!" the girl muttered, "I was just trying to help."

I felt bad and decided to write her a note. What was the worst that could happen? I tore off a piece of paper, and wrote:

"I'm sorry for that. I'm not usually that mean. If you have lunch period five like me, maybe I can explain.
Jasleen."

I leaned over and put the note on her desk. She wrote back.

"K. Meet me @ caf 4.
Gianna (Gigi)"

* * *

Four periods later, in cafeteria four I searched for this Gigi girl. I found her talking to a girl near the lunch line.

"Oh, hey, Jasleen!" Gigi said. "I was just talking to Tyra. Tyra, this is my new friend, Jasleen. Jasleen, this is my best friend, Tyra."

"Nice to meet you!" Tyra said cheerfully. She had huge dimples and freckles and silky shoulder length, burgundy hair.

"I have to buy lunch," I said. "I'll meet you at the table."

"Okay. We're the table diagonally across from the lunch lines, and to the right. Table 10."

I said, "Okay", and walked to the lunch line. I instantly smelled the aroma of something tasty. I walked inside and saw that it was "create your own taco" day. I stuffed my taco shell. This was a lot better than the tofu meatloaf that tasted like barf and plastic from move number three. Now this, I could get used to. I paid with my lunch money, said thank you, and went to look for Gigi.

When I started to follow her directions, I spotted her from behind, recognizing her long, jet black hair, sitting at a different table from where she'd told me she'd be. I went up to her and tapped her on the shoulder.

"I didn't know you changed tables." I said, trying to take a seat next to her.

She turned around, but it was not Gigi. The girl looked me up and down with disapproval.

"Sorry!" I said, feeling my face turn red. "I thought you were Gigi."

"Wait, you freaking spaz!" I didn't have to turn around to know who said that.

Surely she couldn't be talking to me. I wasn't the one with everything hanging out of my tight shirt. I wasn't wearing a shirt designed and sized for my baby sister. I didn't look like I belonged in a club! I spotted Gigi, and not wanting to have a detention on my first day, I went over to her, and sat down quickly.

"I thought I saw you at another table. Your hair looks so much like that girl's over there." When I pointed at the girl, she was still staring at me.

Gigi laughed and said, "Looks like you got someone's attention."

"So," Tyra said, "did you really move six times?"

"Yeah." I took a bite of my taco. "But, I'm nothing like you have heard. I might have a bad rep, but I can be very nice." I looked down in my juice. "I'm just trying to fit in, you know?"

They were silent.

"Jasleen, mind if I call you Jas? I have a thing for nicknames."

"She does," said Tyra. "I'm Ty, and she's Gigi instead of Gianna!"

"Sure," I said. I kind of liked the sound of Jas.

Gigi smiled. "Anyway *Jas*, you don't have to fit in. If people don't want to accept the real you, they don't know what they are missing." Ty nodded in agreement. "Besides, we did the same thing when we were new. We almost got suspended."

"Yolo," Tyra said. "We got into a cat fight. This girl tried to-"

"Spaz!" Anastasia shouted. The girl I'd confused Gigi with approached me right next to her. "I called you. You better answer me, you fat pig! You need to learn the rules!" She took her homemade sushi rolls with soy sauce and flung it towards my face. Fortunately, she had bad aim and it landed on my shirt.

The cafeteria froze in amazement.

"No!" I stood up. "You need to learn the rules. Are you done with that?" I asked this boy at the table next to mine, looking at his huge serving of lasagna. I didn't wait for an answer but thanked him anyway, and dumped it all over her ponytail. I rubbed the sauce in to make sure that it had all gotten on her hair.

At first she just stared at me, her gray eyes popping out of cinnamon colored skin. Then she cried of embarrassment. Just then, Anastasia appeared and took out her phone and speed dialed her father.

Gigi and Ty stared at me wide-eyed, while Gigi whispered, "Her father is Principal King."

"Daddy! We have a situation! Jasleen Tyler just threw food at me!" She paused. "But, Daddy! Fine! I'll do it myself!" She slammed her iPhone down on our table. She started to charge at me, but she fell down. Tyra had tripped her.

Gigi grabbed Tyra's hand. Tyra grabbed mine, and we ran together out of the cafeteria cracking up.

"You're so fat!" Anastasia cried out. "You'll never win the contest!" Everyone continued to laugh hysterically. She ran by us, the sauce dripping from her hair.

She was right in a way. How would I win with excess weight that I carried? I wasn't that fat, but I still needed to lose the weight. I needed to win. Maybe God was trying to tell me something. This was a better time to prove to Anastasia and my dad that I could be pretty and I could win this contest. I couldn't wait to see Anastasia's face when I took her down!

* * *

Every day, I skipped breakfast and lunch. I thought that it was the quickest way to lose weight. I would get terrible pains in my stomach, but I kept reminding myself that victory would be sweeter than any food. I did my best to hide that I was starving. On Saturday night at dinner, I gave my dog most of my chili. All was going perfectly, until Jocelyn bent down to tie her shoe.

"Dad, why is Max eating chili?" Jocelyn asked.

Shut up. Shut up. Shut up. Shut up.

"I have no idea." He bent down to look. "Jade can't get out of her highchair. So…" He sat back up and looked at me. Why did I always get accused first?

"Jasleen, why didn't you eat your chili?" Mom asked.

I tried to think of an excuse that was good enough to end the conversation. "Not that it wasn't good mom, but um…I'm not hungry."

"Jasween gave me samwish," Jade spoke certainly. Mom looked confused.

"Why didn't you eat your lunch?" Jo asked me. All eyes were puncturing a whole through my face.

This was too much. Feeling cornered, I stood up, pushed in my chair and ran upstairs.

I jumped on my bed and turned on my iHome's radio to 102.1, and "Titanium" by David Guetta started blasting out of the speakers. Usually, I would attempt to sing the lyrics, but today I just sat and stared at the wall. Someone knocked at the door. I turned the music off.

"Jasleen, can I come in?" Jo asked.

"It's a free country" I said, turning my back to the door.

"I'll take that as a yes." She sat on my bed. "How come you won't eat?"

"I don't know."

"I'm not Mom or Dad. I know that you haven't eaten properly in two weeks."

"I eat Special K breakfast bars!" I said defensively. She gave me this disappointed look. "Besides, how would you know?"

"I know people. Gigi's sister, Claudia, is in my French class. She tells me what Gigi tells her."

"Big mouth," I muttered.

"I heard that." she said. "She also tells me that you are going to be in a fashion competition. You are trying to lose weight, aren't you?"

"Yeah, but it's none of your business! I know what you are going to say." I raised the pitch of my voice imitating her. "Jasleen!" I dramatically sighed. "You can't be hurting yourself! Trust me, I went through the same thing three years ago when I was your age. I didn't get called back for the show 'Pretty Little Liars.'" I went back to my regular voice. "Could *you* have really gone through anything worse than breaking your perfect nails?" I spat.

"Ok. I have no clue what your problem is, but all I want to do is help." She waited for me to respond, but I didn't say anything. "Fine…don't expect me to pick you back up when you hurt yourself."

"I won't, because I don't want you to show me how to be a perfect suck up just like you!"

"Don't say I never warned you." She slammed my door, walked to her room, and slammed her door.

I didn't mean to hurt her feelings. Maybe I should stop this crash diet. What was I thinking? I couldn't stop now. But that chili looked so good. *Snap out of it*, I told myself.

I decided to go to bed. I couldn't face the fact that I was slowly digging myself into a deep hole.

* * *

On Tuesday, Gigi had lost all confidence in me. She told me that I needed to get help and basically kicked me out from our lunch table. She called what I was doing disgusting. I called it redemption. With nowhere to go, I went to my locker and leaned on it.

"Jasleen, you are beautiful!" Jo had said. "Jasleen, you…are beautiful," Dad had said.

All of sudden the room started spinning and the floor met my face as I drifted into a deep sleep.

* * *

"Jas! Please wake up! Please!" I heard a voice cry.

I slowly opened my eyes. I was on a bed in a dimly lit hospital room, surrounded by stuffed animals and 'get well soon' cards.

"Wha.." I tried to lift my head, which only resulted in a headache.

"Oh my gosh. Thank you, God! Oh Jas, you fainted at school! The paramedics brought you here after you were found unconscious.

What?

"I…" I didn't know what to say.

"Shhh!" Jocelyn said. "Dad's calling his boss to tell him he can't go to work today, and Mom's getting a coffee from the Starbucks downstairs. Dad left you these." She pointed to a bouquet of flowers on the windowsill. She took my hand. "He's really sorry, Jas." After a moment of silence, I looked up at Tyra and Gigi. "Oh! I forgot to tell you, Tyra and Gigi came by to see you after school. I'll leave you all to talk."

"Thanks, Jocelyn." I whispered hoarsely. "I really didn't mean to say what I did on Saturday."

"And I didn't mean it when I said that I would stop helping you. You know I'll always be there for you." She kissed my forehead. Jo left the room, and Gigi and Tyra ran up to my bed.

"Jasleen, I am really sorry I left you. Please forgive me. I just didn't realize how serious your problem was. I should've helped you!"

"Yeah. I'm sorry too," Tyra said. "I should've forced you to eat."

"Don't blame yourselves." I said. "I didn't know that this would happen.

"You're gonna make me cry." Gigi said.

"It's fine. Thanks for caring." For a moment we just smiled at each other, taking in what just happened.

"Now, enough of this mushy moment! We have to shop, pretty soon." Tyra's face lit up. "But more importantly Jas, you have to swear on…" She paused and picked up a copy of Seventeen Magazine on the side table. "…Harry Styles that you will eat from now on!"

"Do you really expect me to swear on One Direction?" I asked her.

"Just do it!" Gigi said.

"Fine." I placed my hand on the cover of Seventeen. "I promise to take care of myself. No more crazy clothes or crash diets." I said.

"And…" Gigi pressed.

"And what?" I asked stupidly. She hit my leg.

"And, I am NOT fat!"

"JASLEEN IS NOT FAT!" Tyra declared. We all started laughing. Things were going to be okay.

* * *

On Thursday, when I was released, I made plans to meet up with Gigi and Tyra at the King of Prussia mall for the following week. Since Ms. Jones said we could work in groups, of course we would work together. There would be five scenes consisting of sporty, neon, metallic, going green, and career. Tyra, Gigi, and I were against Anastasia, Janice, and Samantha for our age division.

We decided to go to Forever 21 for the sporty scene. In the store disco balls hung and Justin Timberlake's latest hit was blasting from the speakers. I stopped in front of an orange basketball jersey, made feminine with gold and purple stripes.

"Yuck!" we said in unison.

"I'll buy you that for Christmas this year!" Gigi told Tyra. We started laughing. "Seriously. It would look good with your gold Sperrys." She paused, giving us a serious expression. We frowned, but then she started laughing again, and so did we.

Tyra stopped in front of a mannequin wearing a tennis set. She found one in pastel green, including a spandex and nylon shirt with a spandex miniskirt. Gigi found one in pastel blue, and I found one in pastel lavender. The three of us also found pastel colored tennis racquets in the nearby sporting goods store to match our outfits.

We needed shoes. We walked into Famous Footwear and ended up finding really cute tennis shoes. We also bought the same white Under Armor knapsacks to finish it off. We were off to a pretty good start.

After paying, we went to Wet Seal for our going green scene. I saw a hunter green halter dress with a brown beaded neckline, and I decided that it would look stunning with silver t-strap sandals and silver accessories.

"Cute! I love the colors. Let's take it," Tyra said.

"I love your style." Gigi said.

I found the same dress in sea green for Tyra, and the same one for Gigi in a

dark, spring green. This was really easy, and it was also so much fun! My confidence really helped me to see that under that make up, I could actually be…pretty.

We checked out *579* for the neon scene. Tyra saw a black t-shirt in the back of the store with a picture of lips in the center filled with neon colored dots.

"Wow, this is nice!" I said.

"Well, for 30 bucks it's not *that* nice!" Tyra said.

"Relax, Ty. It's called allowance! It's all covered," Gigi said.

"Who's your father like the president? How much money do you get for allowance?" I asked suspiciously.

"Ok. You caught me. Most of it is from babysitting," she confessed.

"I thought so."

We found the shirts in three sizes, but the extra larges were gone. It was fine for Gigi and Tyra, who were extra smalls, but not for me. They tried them on, while I just watched pitifully.

"We look hot!" Gigi said.

"You do, but I don't." I said. "What am I supposed to wear, a paper sack?"

"Oh, hush!" Tyra said walking to the racks behind me. "Try this on!"

"But, it's only a medium. I can't fit in that!"

"Try it on, gosh!" Gigi said.

I walked to the dressing room and tried on the shirt. OH MY GOSH! It fit me! When I was discharged from the hospital, I promised to eat a balanced diet, and it worked. Wow! I practically ran out of the dressing room to where I found the girls talking. I slowly walked out towards them.

"Yeah, and my mom said, like no way, and…," Gigi said.

"Oh my gosh! Look at Jas!" Tyra said cheerfully.

I spun around. "Work it!" Gigi said smiling. "I knew you could do it."

"You look awesome." Tyra agreed.

"Thank you, thank you!" I took a dramatic bow. I was beaming.

"Ok. It's 5:15. If we're done shopping by 6:15, we can get a pretzel and leave by 6:30. Then, we can all make it home in time for tonight's episode of *Pretty Little Liars*," Gigi said. "Ok, we don't have a lot of time left! We need leggings and shoes and necklaces."

"Got it!" I said pointing to a rack of leggings.

"Those are cute," Tyra said, holding a pair of leggings with rhinestones throughout.

We agreed, and she bought me a medium pair in neon green, a neon yellow pair for Gigi, and a neon pink pair for herself. I picked out multicolored, beaded neon necklaces, and we bought them along with black high-heeled, glossy ankle boots.

We tried Joyce Leslie for the metallic scene. We were greeted by loud music.

"Sorry for Party Rockin'," Gigi sang. "Look over there! That vest is nice."

We all agreed that the lightly sequined blazer was perfect. Tyra picked out plain black shirts to go underneath.

"Now all we need are shoes and jeans," Tyra said. I picked out shiny silver metallic jeggings. They weren't over the top, and they were very tasteful.

"Those jeggings are really cute," Gigi said.

"Should we try the Guess for shoes?" I asked.

"Sure!" Tyra said, paying with her gold Visa.

We walked out with our bags that weighed a ton.

"Maybe we should stop. These bags are getting pretty heavy," I suggested. We thought about it for a moment and then started laughing.

We entered the Guess and found the cutest pair of shoes on display.

"Wow, I love these metallic silver mesh combat boots!" I said.

"Me, too." They agreed.

We found our sizes and I paid for them. "My treat," I said.

"Thanks, Jas!" Tyra laughed.

"One more scene." Gigi said, sighing. She flipped her wavy black hair and put it in a high ponytail.

"Thank you, God! My feet hurt," Tyra said.

We walked into New York & Company for the career scene. We decided to be business women. After browsing for a while, we finally found an age appropriate suit.

"What color? Should we get brown, black, or what?" Gigi asked.

"What about if you get all white, I get all black, and Gigi gets black with white pin stripes?" Tyra asked.

"That'd be nice, right Jas?"

"I think so, too," I said.

"Well, what about shoes?" Tyra asked.

We turned around and found a pair of dreamy black heels. Jocelyn had told me before that heels boosted your posture and your confidence. For the first time, I was actually starting to believe her. With a black briefcase matching our shoes and pinstriped 'Alicia Keys' styled fedoras, we were going to be great.

"Let's celebrate with smoothies," Tyra said. "My treat!" We all slapped fives and walked to Smoothie Paradise. We ordered three tropical smoothies and sat down at a nearby table. Guess who just happened to be walking by? Anastasia and her clan. Wonderful…

"Seriously?" Gigi said, responding to Anastasia's pink crop top and studded nose ring. Surprise, surprise.

Janice spotted me and whispered to Anastasia. I never liked that girl. Anastasia, Janice, and Samantha strutted towards us.

"Well, well, well, if it isn't slime balls numbers 1, 2 and 3." Anastasia flipped her hair.

"Well, well, well, if it isn't the wannabe *ladies*," I said, looking at Samantha and Janice. "And the *tramp*?" I looked at Anastasia.

"Oh! I love that movie, *Lady and the Tramp*!" Samantha shouted. She was as dumb as a stump.

"Uh… anyway," Anastasia said with her valley girl voice. "You better watch your back, pig face. It's gonna be a long Saturday! I wish you all luck, because uh… you're gonna need it." Anastasia winked and the three of them turned together like a school of fish.

"Ladies!" Anastasia snapped her manicured fingers.

They started walking away

"Whatever!" Gigi said. If she felt intimidated, she didn't have a hard time hiding it. I on the other hand couldn't stop my palms from sweating.

* * *

"Lights, camera, action!" Ms. Jones shouted on Saturday to open the show. "I'm so pleased with my girls for volunteering to help the Clothes for Caring foundation!" She paused until everyone stopped clapping. "So please give everyone the respect that they deserve! Enjoy! Thank you!" She turned off the microphone and after a blackout the curtains opened and "Scream and Shout" by Britney Spears started playing. Strobe lights came on and the first group of girls started modeling. I left the side of the stage and met Gigi and Tyra in the makeup room to get ready for the sporty scene in the 14-16 age division.

The night before, Jocelyn had showed me ways to lighten my makeup so it wouldn't be too much. So, on Tyra and Gigi, I used light lime green eye shadow, black mascara, blush, and dark red lipstick. Gigi put my hair into a tight braid as I had done with hers and Tyra's. We used black bracelets to tie the ends, and we were done. We slipped into our outfits and waited for our turn.

"Gigi's group, now!" Ms. Jones said through her earpiece backstage.

We walked up the stairs and the lights followed us. It was amazing. We walked sophisticatedly with Gigi in the middle and Tyra and I on the sides. The crowd was going crazy and I heard my name being yelled by Jo. We got to the end of the runway, posed and smiled for the camera, and rotated positions. Now I was in the middle and Gigi and Tyra traded sides. We walked back, posed another time and exited.

"Wow! That was great." Gigi yelled as soon as we got backstage.

"Shhh, Gigi!" yelled Ms. Jones.

"Sorry."

As soon as we got to the dressing rooms, we started jumping up and down.

"That was awesome!" I shouted.

"It was!" Tyra squealed.

"Let's get ready. The green scene is next." Gigi said. She opened the curtain where our clothes were hanging and gasped.

"Oh my gosh!" I shouted.

Our dresses were ripped to shreds at the top, and the heels had red dots of permanent marker all over them. I could only imagine who had done it. Anastasia.

"This is the last straw!" I shouted, "If she wants to fight dirty, two can play that game." I said, marching to the door. Knowing her personality, she had probably done this because our outfits were similar to her group's.

"No!" Gigi caught me. "You can't! If you do this, you would be playing just as dirty as those stupid girls." I turned around.

"We can make them our own," Tyra said confidently. "You know, be original!"

"Okay" I agreed, not feeling very confident. We put on our torn dresses, and they didn't look so bad. Tyra was right, they were unique.

We walked, not sure of what we were going to do, backstage. When it was our turn, we walked up the steps, took a deep breath, and started walking, focusing straight ahead. At first the audience was puzzled, but then they started applauding! Soon, we realized that Anastasia, Janice, and Samantha had similar dresses that were normal, but ours were different. The crowd loved them, so we smiled confidently. We posed and walked back down the runway. For the next scenes, the audience members were bored out of their minds for every group but ours. During the metallic scene, the audience applauded our style. They didn't clap for Anastasia's group! Next was the neon scene, in which received a standing ovation for our shirts and accessories. The audience loved our individuality, and we loved their enthusiasm.

I was so proud of myself for finally being confident. I actually felt beautiful, and I could not remember the last time I felt that way. I felt so positive, like the weight of the world was lifted off my shoulders. I felt free.

The last scene was the career scene. Gigi, Tyra, and I walked with our briefcases, backstage. We took our places on the stage, and strutted down the runway. In the middle of the runway, we put our briefcases down, sat on them, got up, switched positions, and grabbed the briefcase in front of us. The crowd erupted, and we smiled. We posed for the last time and took our place among the groups for the interviewing segment.

Every group had to answer three questions about life, and the groups would keep rotating until it was their turn. After what felt like hours of smiling and waiting for the groups to finish, it was Anastasia's group's turn. Her group took their place on the center of the runway.

"Anastasia," Ms. Jones said. "What is the most important aspect of life?"

"Me, duh!" Anastasia said, rolling her eyes. The audience gasped. She smacked her gum and flipped her hair.

"You don't think that uh… anything else is important?" Ms. Jones asked nervously.

"Um, can you hear or are you deaf?! I said…me! I'm the most important aspect of life. Gosh these people."

The silent crowd turned into a chaotic scene as everyone started talking with disbelief. When the crowd got quiet again, Ms. Jones continued. "Janice, dear, who do you admire?"

"Myself, of course! Like, who wouldn't?" Samantha and Anastasia high fived. The audience started whispering.

"And Samantha, what is your definition of beautiful?"

"Gawd! Don't you, like, know anything? Being beautiful is when you're so hot that people ask you, 'are you like the sun, or something?-Because the room is feeling warmer! And being beautiful is like being skinny. You have to have like lipo…. and-"

"Samantha! We are running out of time, sorry. That was group 26, everyone!" The audience didn't applaud until we took the stage.

"Gigi, Jasleen, and Tyra, please take the stage!" Ms. Jones said happily. "It's great to see you!"

"It's great to see you, too!" we answered. Tyra took the second microphone.

"Tyra, what is the most important thing in life?" Ms. Jones asked.

"I believe school is the most important thing in life because without it you couldn't learn about what it takes to be successful!" Tyra smiled.

The audience applauded.

"Gigi, who do admire, dear?"

"I admire my parents because they put up with me!" The audience started laughing. "Seriously! They help me through everything. I don't know what I'd do without their support!"

"I love you, Gianna!" her parents shouted from the audience.

"And, Jasleen, what is your definition of beautiful?"

I took a deep breath. "Being beautiful is being a role model, helping others, and caring for others. Being beautiful is not about what's outside, but rather, what's within!"

The audience started to applaud, and my father stood up and clapped. For a split second, I realized that this was the proudest moment of my life.

"Thank you, girls!" Ms. Jones said over the applause. After four more groups were interviewed, she said, "That's it. It's voting time."

While all the contestants filed on stage, the ballots were collected from the judges.

"Well, this is it!" I said to Tyra and Gigi. "Now, I really do understand the definition of beautiful!"

"You are that definition!" Gigi said hugging me. We all held hands.

"Thank you, guys, for everything." I said.

"The votes are in!" Ms. Jones said. "For ages 10-13, the winners are…" She unfolded the paper. "Group 14. Brielle, Maria, Logan, and Brianna. Congratulations!" They stepped forward and received a $200 check. "I'll reveal ages 17-20 first since the 14-16 division is receiving a special award. For 17- 20, the winners are…" She unfolded the paper. "Group 21, Melinda, Shaniya, Karen, and I'Donia. Congratulations!" The audience clapped as they received a check for $200. "And lastly for the ages of 14-16… drum roll please…"

Anastasia and her crew stepped forward and curtseyed before the winner was even announced.

"Thank you all!" Anastasia bowed. "We love you all!

Ms. Jones rolled her eyes and continued. "Group 27, Jasleen, Tyra, and Gigi, who are also winners of the first ever, 'Miss Classy Award'!"

"Oh my gosh. What the heck!" Anastasia cried out. "This is mine, mine, MINE!"

The crowd went wild as the three of us shouted, jumped, and hugged. We all agreed to a

slumber party at Gigi's later to celebrate. I started to cry as I was handed a $300 check. I felt really beautiful and I was changed forever that one day. I wanted the whole world to hear that they too, could be beautiful. Everyone has a soul and everyone is beautiful!

"Good night, and thanks for coming!"

The photographer snapped our pictures for the newspaper as we posed with our check and our plaque.

* * *

"Stunning!" my mom squealed. "Amazing!" She wrapped me in a tight hug. "Oh, look at my beautiful baby!" She squeezed me tighter.

"Uh, Mom it's my turn," Jo said. "Come 'ere!" She gave me a hug. "The boys better watch out," she whispered. I giggled.

"Pwetty, mommy! Look at pwetty Jwaslee!" Jade said, pointing at me and jumping at my feet. I picked her up.

"Thank you, Jade!"

"Uh… Jasleen, can we talk?" my dad asked.

"Sure," I said, giving Jade to Jocelyn.

We went outside and sat by the water fountains.

"Honey, I'm really sorry for making you feel insecure. I didn't mean to compare you to Jocelyn. I love you so much that I guess

I wanted you to change into something else to be accepted in today's world. But now I see you had already done that. I realize that I was changing you for me, and not for the world. But I have to tell you, you are so beautiful today, and every day. The way the light shines in your eyes is beautiful, and it reminds me of your mom so much! Please forgive me, Jas. Please. I'll really change. I promise. I don't want our relationship to be this way." He pinched my cheeks. "You really became a young woman today, Jasleen. You keep being you because in the end, that's all that counts!"

He smiled, and for the first time I knew that he really meant it. *I am beautiful.*

He hugged and squeezed me tightly.

"I love you, Dad!"

"I love you too, Jasleen." He said. And the ending felt like a fairytale.

Dear Diary,

Today I learned what the word beautiful really means. I spent so much time trying to fit in, that I didn't respect myself. Wearing weird clothes that didn't fit my body, obsessing about my odd hair, and trying to be weird and tough, was not beautiful and it wasn't me. I learned that everyone is beautiful in their own way. God made our world to be this way. Being different helps us to learn about each other. Well, gotta go. I'm at Gigi's house at our sleepover, and we don't plan on sleeping at all! Gigi just threw popcorn in my face, so it's on!

I Am Beautiful: But the LORD said unto Samuel, Look not on his countenance, or on the height of his stature; because I have refused him: for the LORD seeth not as man seeth; for man looketh on the outward appearance, but the LORD looketh on the heart.

- I Samuel 16:7

I Am Strong

"Come on, Arianna," Carrie said. "You're going to miss the votes."

"Carrie, hold your horses. I'm not going to miss it!" I said.

Today was the last theme day of spirit week. Every day of the week students would dress up for a specific theme. Then, every morning of the day each homeroom would vote to see what boy and girl showed the most school spirit. Every day of spirit week, I came in dreaded second place to the most popular girl in 10th grade, Rebekah Larson.

Monday's theme was 'Red Carpet Day'. Tuesday was 'Year 3000 Day.' Wednesday was 'Sports Day.' Thursday was '60's Day.' Friday was 'Caribbean Day'. Even the rowdy boys dressed up, eager to win the $50 gift card that the winners got along with Broadway tickets that were raffled off.

Today, I was ready! No one could beat my Caribbean pink halter dress with strappy pink sandals. I was also wearing designer sunglasses and a clear beach bag, including a hat and sunscreen. My outfit looked better than Rebekah's lime green sundress with gold flip flops and a white scarf. Being a competitor, I hated losing. Today, Rebekah was going down.

"Class, please take your seats. As usual, we have a lot of things to take care of, starting with the homeroom votes for Caribbean Day!" Mrs. Smith smiled. "Ladies, take the stage!"

My heart pounded as I walked to the front of the classroom with Jessica, Michelle, Kim, Mary, Carrie, Ariel, Nora, and Crystal. My mind was focused on the gift card and the *Wicked* Broadway show tickets that would be raffled off to the day's winners.

"Girls, turn so everyone can see your outfits," Mrs. Smith said. All of the girls turned in a slow rotation. Then we all faced the back wall. Even though I was facing the wall, I could see what was happening with the votes through the reflection of the T.V. Mrs. Smith pointed towards me and five hands went up. Megan, Celeste, Tom, Trish, and Brad voted for me. I frowned. Bekah got 10 votes.

"Rebekah, you're our winner!" Mrs. Smith announced.

My jaw dropped. Surely, that couldn't be right. I was furious! Bekah said, "Oh, thank you," took a bow, then, swinging her hips, sauntered out the door.

* * *

Two periods later, when I was at my locker, Nora stopped me.

"Ari, as much as I should just keep my mouth shut, I can't. I didn't want to be the one to tell you this, but, I know it's only right that I tell you-"

"Tell me what?" I interrupted.

Nora sighed. "This morning Abby told everyone that you weren't nearly as pretty as Bekah."

"So?"

"She told everyone not to vote for you. She said that you could never beat Bekah in anything. She said you were ugly, poor, and your clothes came from bins. I'm so sorry... She also said that you were jealous of Bekah and you always wanted attention." The bell rang. "Gotta go. Sorry again. I just thought you should know," Nora said.

If I thought that I was angry before, it was nothing compared to how I felt after I heard that gossip. Rebekah changed in the worst way. She used to be my best friend. We used to do everything together. A year ago, she became jealous of me after Alex, a boy she liked, became one of my best friends. It was all downhill from there, and I discovered that she could be mean and nasty when she wanted to be. I knew she put Abby up to it, but I never expected her to sink so low. Bekah knew how much I wanted those tickets for my mom's birthday because I couldn't afford them. I ran to the bathroom, looking for Bekah.

"What's your problem?" I shouted. "You know how much I wanted those tickets!"

"Whatever." she said, reapplying makeup to her face. "You can have them! I only wanted them to take Alex to NYC for our six month anniversary, but the sweetheart said he was throwing me a party instead. He wanted to step up our, uh, relationship. I totally considered inviting you." She said sarcastically. "So it looks like I won't be needing these!"

I gasped.

She took the tickets from her purse and held them out in front of me. I reached for them, but she tripped me causing my head to fall into the sink, which was filled with dirty, cold water. I grabbed my traveling cup from my bag, filling it with what seemed like sludge, and threw it at her face. All of her makeup came running down and her hair was soaked.

"What's your problem?!" she exploded.

"Oops!" I squealed.

She slapped my face.

I punched her nose.

She put her hands over my eyes.

I pulled her hair.

We fought and fought. Soon a crowd was gathered in the bathroom shouting, "Fight! Fight!"

All of a sudden, a whistle blew. Mrs. Askan, our principal, stood over us.

"Arianna and Rebekah! What is going on?" she bellowed. The bathroom went silent as the kids quickly dispersed.

"In my office…NOW!"

"Gosh, touchy touchy, Mrs. A!" Rebekah snorted as she got up and tried to straighten her dress.

"Ms. Turner, call these girls' parents. They were fighting!" Mrs. Askan ordered as we stepped into the office. She looked down at me through her huge glasses. "We have a case 219."

Ms. Turner nodded and tapped the keys on the keyboard, most likely researching our parents' phone numbers.

"You were fighting," Mrs. Askan said, as if we hadn't already established this. "As you know, we have a no- tolerance policy for fighting here at Caper High school. I don't want to hear your false tales. I want the truth. Since you are equally in trouble, and I can pull the bathroom tapes to find out the truth, I want to hear some clarity right this instant!"

"The truth is," Bekah began.

"The truth is," I said.

"She is jealous of me!"

"She was talking about me!" I interjected.

"She clobbered me!!"

"She stole my tickets!"

"I won them fairly!"

"She tripped me."

Mrs. Askan was scribbling in her notepad.

"She threw disgusting water on my face….WATER on *my* face!"

"She slapped me!" I said.

Bekah rolled her eyes at my accusation. "She punched me!"

"She's a punk!"

"She's a jealous cow, and she's a boyfriend stealer."

"He wasn't taken!"

"Both of you shut your mouths!" Mrs. Askan barked. She smoothed out her skirt. "Both of you, detention with me for two weeks after school! And one day of in-school suspension."

"But, I have cheerleading practice!" Rebekah whined.

"In that case, a week suspension looks great, too." Mrs. Askan warned.

"I'm good!" she exclaimed.

I was too speechless. What would my stepmother say? Meredith would rip my head off, for sure.

"As well, you will both receive ten demerits, and your parents will be called.'"

"But-," I protested.

"You two back to class! But first fix yourselves. Arianna go to the west bathroom, Bekah the east."

"But," we both said in unison. We both knew we had unfinished business to take care of.

"Go!"

We got up and walked our separate ways. She sauntered like everything was fine. "Hey, Jason!" she called out. Even at our lowest points, we still weren't equal.

* * *

"Beep! Beep! Beep! Beep!" The alarm went off as I entered my house. I punched in the code and the house went silent. Automatically, I knew my 18 year-old, redheaded stepsister, Reid, was at lacrosse practice. That was good because I needed some time to think. I took some carrots out of the refrigerator and sat down. I found the Post-its that Meredith was famous for. To my dad, she used her lovely stationery with Meredith Virginia Greene beautifully printed on them. My dad's note said she'd be home soon, and that tonight was his night. Gag! My note, on the invisible side of the fridge in plain white said clean up the kitchen and make dinner before she come home, or else. Man, I was sick of her. I wish she'd just win the lottery and take her Prada butt away from my daddy. But Reid could stay. She hated her mom like I did, and we had similar thoughts.

I needed to get away. If I stayed, by the time she heard Ms. Turner's message, World War III would begin! Of course, when she moved in she brought along her phone answering machine that needed a password to delete the messages. "For us, Victor," she had said, giving my father a kiss while shooting me a look. She meant for me, so she'd have access to her cousin's stepmother, a.k.a, Mrs. Askan.

I got a Post-it out of my bag. I scribbled, 'Meredith, I'm at Carrie's house,' imagining the twisted look she'd give when she read it. It didn't matter. I had to get away. I stuck it on the refrigerator and left.

I ran three houses down and rang the doorbell. Carrie's careless older brother answered the door, letting me in. I ran past Carrie's lazy dog. Carrie was doing her homework, but when she saw the tears in my eyes, she dropped her pencil and ran to me. I told her everything, about what Abby and Bekah had done. Then I told her about the fight, and my worries about how Meredith would react.

"You can't cry, Ari," Carrie said. "That's what Bekah wants you to do. Just don't worry. Pray. Besides God will get her back for wasting all of those tissues for you know what." She smiled. "She's as fake as a Barbie!"

We both cracked up, and when she snorted, the laughter grew. With her own charm she had made her point. I shouldn't be crying,

I was calmed down when Carrie agreed that we should do our homework together for that night. And since her mom wouldn't be home for another three hours, we ordered a medium extra cheesy pizza from Papa John's. We had so much fun that I had forgotten about the day's events. Eventually, though, I had to go home.

* * *

When I arrived home, Reid was talking on her iPhone.

"Yeah, Mom," she said. "She just walked in." She took the phone off of her ear. "She wants to know if you made dinner for us." I gave her a pleading look. "Actually, she ordered Chinese," she said.

I gave her a look of gratitude. "Yeah, it's the low fat steamed chicken, and no she didn't order those carb loaded rolls," Reid explained with her signature eye roll. "Ok, Ok, yeah, yeah, sure."

"Smooches!" I heard Meredith shriek.

"Yeah, smooches," Reid mumbled. She hung up. "Geez! I thought she'd never shut up!" We laughed.

I stopped laughing and said, "Wait. How are you going to get that order here in ten minutes?"

"I know a guy," she said seriously. "Really! You know Helen's bro, Wade?"

I nodded. "He works at the Chinese Palace," she said, matter-of-factly.

"God bless you!" I pretended to bow at her.

"The trick to mother Meredith is to charm her!" Reid could never call Meredith by her first name to her face, ever. She threw me an apple and turned back to her AP calculus homework.

I decided to take a bath. It always helped me to relax. When I came out of the bathroom, I heard the opening front door echo. It was Wade. I heard Reid laugh at something Wade said, but then stop. That's when I heard the garage door open. I could hear her chasing Wade out the back door. Man, she was so cool.

* * *

"Reid!" Meredith called. Reid flew down the stairs.

"Yes, Mom."

"Reid, where's the scum?" Meredith gave her a look that showed how painful it was for her to acknowledge my existence. I don't know what she expected. When you marry someone, you are expected to marry their family as well.

A half an hour later, we were in Meredith's Porsche ready to go to New York. We stopped in Dunkin Donuts, and she let me order whatever I wanted. I ordered a strawberry iced doughnut while she sipped on her iced coffee. We sat and she asked me to tell her about the fight.

"Well, first of all, did you win?" she asked excitedly.

"Well…I won ten demerits!" I exclaimed sarcastically.

"You know those snotty Larsons. Her older sister, Gloria, a senior, is just like her!"

I laughed imagining an older Rebekah. "You know, you shouldn't have been fighting. You know that God wouldn't want you fighting unless it was self-defense."

"She knew that I wanted those tickets, and she purposely dropped them in that sink! She knows that my mom has been struggling by herself and couldn't buy tickets, and she still messed with me."

"Honey, sometimes we have to turn the other cheek."

"Reid, Mom's been talking about seeing that show since last year. I wanted to give her those tickets so badly. I want to turn her cheeks with my fist… I am pathetic," I said.

"You're right!"

"Gee, thanks."

"You're right for saying that you are pathetic. Look at you! You are eating yourself alive."

"That's true."

"You're telling me! Your eyes are so puffy that you look like you've been through a wind tunnel!"

"You are so mean." I playfully slapped her arm.

"I know!"

We ate in silence for a while.

"Now, let's get going, she said. We have a fun day ahead of us tomorrow."

We walked back to the car, and I fell asleep happily for the first time in weeks.

* * *

I woke up to hear *Right Now* by Rihanna blasting loudly through the car speakers. Reid was singing loudly with the radio. She started tapping the steering wheel to the beat, but then stopped when she looked over at me. "Hey, sleepy head!

I sat up stretching, sure that I was smelling something delicious.

"I got you the new bacon burger from Wendy's, the one that you like!"

"Thanks," I said, yawning. "What time is it?"

"12 A.M." She said coolly. "We'll be there in about 15 minutes."

"Where are we staying?"

"Only the best for my step sis! We'll be staying at the Trump Plaza!"

"Fancy, fancy!"

"Keisha's sister, Sage, is the manager." Leave it to Reid to have every connection in the book. "Anyways, here we are," she sang in a high-pitched voice. We got off the exit and four miles down was the luxurious Trump Plaza.

When we pulled up, the parking attendant got in and parked the car. We walked through the huge gold doors, to the main desk and checked in.

"Hey Saaage!" Reid said to the woman who was wearing a navy blue pantsuit and sitting behind a large desk. "Room for Reynolds!"

"That's room 5169 on floor number five!"

"Thanks!" The lady gave Reid two room keys. Reid gave one to me. "Don't lose it," she said seriously. Everything was dead silent. Then she started cracking up. We turned around. I caught a strong whiff of her Vera Wang perfume as we went up the elevator. Once on floor five, we found our room and Reid unlocked the door, which opened to a huge suite fit for queens. The room was painted a plush lilac, and the beds were huge.

"So, what do you want to do now?" Reid asked casually.

"Go to bed."

"Come on, you party pooper. Stop moping!" She slapped my arm playfully. "I'll order some apple cider!" She offered.

"It's 12: 48, you fool," I said.

"So! We are not resting until you feel better, my love." Reid ran to the phone and called for room service.

She started jumping on the bed, and I shook my head in disapproval. Reid yelled, "Cheer up!" She dragged me on top of a bed and made me stand up. "Jump." she commanded. I bounced and she shouted, "Now."

"The people in the next room are gonna call security because of you!"

"Until you smile, I don't care!"

I faked a smile.

"I don't appreciate the forced smile, Arianna Penelope!"

I finally gave in and smiled for real.

"Now, that's the Ari that I want."

There was a knock at the door. "Room service!" a male called.

Reid ran to the door and gave him a tip. She took the fancy platter, said thanks, and closed the door.

"Cheers to New York!" she said loudly.

"You are so dumb!" I joked.

"And so are you for not raising your glass!" she joked back.

"Amen." We clanked glasses and drank our apple cider.

Twenty minutes of drinking and jumping later, we hit the sack.
I was really looking forward to the morning!

* * *

"Wake up, Sunshine!" Reid sang. I groaned. "Wakey, wakey!"
She shook me and I finally got up. "We have a swell day ahead of
us, my darling!"

"Where are we going?" I asked excitedly. My sleep seemed to
have changed my demeanor overnight.

"I thought we might eat breakfast in the park, and then go
shopping for your Broadway tickets!"

"Seriously?" I asked.

"Of course!" Reid said. "I thought the three of us might go
for your mom's birthday! It beats giving Meredith her Saturday
facial."

I yawned.

"Wake up!" She threw a pillow square in my face.

"Ow!" I yelled in annoyance.

"Stop whining, and get dressed."

I took a hot shower and threw on my dark American Eagle
jeans, orange t-shirt, and black leather jacket. It took me a
million years to assemble this outfit, while Reid was already
dressed in a pink Hollister shirt, green, white, and pink Hollister
plaid shorts, and green and white sequined heels. She was so
weird, but hey, I loved her for it!

"Ari!"

"What?"

She sang *Starships* while shrugging her shoulders to the imaginary beat of Nicki Minaj's song as we closed our room door and entered the grand hallway.

"Shhh! You're going to wake up the guests!" I said

"Honey! I am a guest too. Ari, Starships were meant to fly!"

I looked at her as if she were an alien. Five minutes later, she was still singing to herself, ignoring the confused looks that people around us were giving her.

* * *

We walked along Times Square while eating breakfast sandwiches. We traveled across the street to Starbucks, and Reid decided to get her usual French vanilla cappuccino. Afterwards, we settled onto a nearby park bench.

"Ahhh!" said Reid, plopping herself down onto a bench. I did the same.

"So what do you think Meredith is doing right now?" I asked.

"Painting her toenails," she said.

"Meredith Virginia Greene paints her own toenails? I'm shocked!"

"She only does on Saturdays."

"Wow, Ms. Greene is a real human being?"

"There's a lot you don't know about Meredith." Reid sipped her coffee. "Ahhhhhh!" she exploded. "This is sooo hot!"

"Idiot."

She slapped my arm.

"What don't I know about your mother?" I asked mid bite of my sandwich.

"Well, you won't believe this, but Mer was in a high school all-girl band!"

"WHAT?"

"Yeah! Spandex and all!"

"What was it called?"

"The Human Hair!"

"You're dead serious?" I asked.

"If I'm lying, God can kill me now."

I burst out with laughter. My insides shook so much and I began to cry.

"So, what did they wear, fake hair or something? Did they dress up like Cindy Lauper?"

"You know how Mer's real hair now is shoulder length? It used to be down to her butt, but now from adding all of those extensions and hair dye when she was in that band, it broke off!" She slapped my thigh. I started laughing all over again. It was so bad that I had to hold on to the railing to stay on the bench.

"Yeah, Mer was cool, but all those years of being single really changed her," Reid said in reflection.

"Yeah! She doesn't dye her hair anymore?" It was my turn to slap Reid's thigh.

"That's not funny!" Reid snapped. She paused to collect herself. "Sorry. It just makes me so upset to remember what happened. It just makes me want to scream!"

"What happened to Meredith?" I asked.

"Three years ago, before she met your dad, Mer was in a terrible relationship with my dad. He was an all-night drinker and well, one night he came home to find divorce papers on his desk." She paused and sipped her coffee slowly, as if to remember something.

"That same night, he came home and punched my mom in the face. She tried to run. But when she got to the steps he... he..."

52

"What?" I asked frightened.

"Scott Greene pushed my six-months pregnant mother down the stairs. She was bruised so badly when I got home from a sleepover the next morning. She was only concerned with one thing, her baby. She kept saying 'my baby' or 'my little girl' and then blacking out. I couldn't drive then. But Arianna, I drove my mom to that hospital that morning prepared to save my soon-to-be little sister. When we got there and the doctors treated my mother, they had announced that the baby did not make it. Believe it or not, the baby was going to be named Penelope after her grandma."

"That makes sense. She kept on calling me 'Penelope', and I got really offended!"

"Now you know why. You see Mer's a human just like the rest of us. After we found out that my father had taken their money and left the country with his mistress, Marcella, she was distraught. She makes mistakes but, in her own way, she just wants you to be happy. She wants you to grow and be her Penelope."

I nodded.

"Do you know what her Penelope would do?"

"What?" I asked.

"Stay strong. Take her madness with gusto, and forgive her. I know it may be rough, but remember, God will fight your battles. Plus, you have me. We just have to be the best Reid and Ari Penelope that we can be. As much as you may disagree sometimes, we have to be more than strong. We must be resilient."

Dear Diary,

Today Meredith, Mom, Reid, and I went to see Wicked. As weird as it was, I was the one who asked Meredith to come. At first when I had asked her, I thought that I must have had a fever. But I eventually realized that God put it on my heart to treat her respectfully. Over the past few days, I have learned to be strong, although I had fought with Bekah. I now understand that Bekah is one of many adversaries that I will encounter in life. I know that I cannot let other people like her dictate my emotions. Through Reid, God showed me that it was okay to make mistakes because he will always be there for me. Here I thought that Meredith would shun me, and I'd be grounded for eternity, but in return for my strength, God gave me the gift of household peace. I guess all you really can do is stay strong, and let God handle your tribulations.

I have to go now because guess what? Family Scrabble night is just minutes away! Mer just might win. From talking to her more, I learned that she and Penelope, her grandmother shared the passion of spelling. She told me that she almost won the national spelling bee! I guess you never really know a person until you make an effort to understand their story.

Ari (Meredith's Penelope)

I Am Strong: *Be strong and of good courage, fear not, nor be afraid of them: for the LORD thy God, he it is that doth go with thee; he will not fail thee, nor forsake thee.*

- DEUTERONOMY 31:6

I Am Forgiving

"Bryn! Bryn!" Bailey jumped up and gave me a hug almost knocking me down.

"Hey, Bails!" I exclaimed. "How was kindergarten?"

"Bryn, today was so fun! We learned how to play the flute for music week!"

"Wow ! You can play the flute?" I asked.

"Uh-huh," she said, smiling.

"Well, come on. Go get your lunchbox." Bailey dashed over to her cubby, took her lunchbox, waved to her teacher, and then we left. After going down two flights of stairs, I led the way outside.

"Guess what?"

"What?" I asked her.

"I made a picture for Mommy today because she looked sad!"

"She's just tired, B."

"Oh." She frowned.

"B-but I'm sure she'll love it!" I quickly added.

"You know what? I wanna make mommy smile! Can I help with dinner?"

"Dinner?" I asked. "And just what exactly do you plan on making?"

"Um…." She thought. "Rice! With broccoli!"

"Rice and broccoli?" I repeated dryly.

"Yeah! I saw it on a cooking show last week. It looked very good, so I want to make it."

"Bailey, not everything that looks delicious on TV is actually good in real life."

"Fine!" She pouted as I took her hand to cross the street.

I thought of Bailey, a five-year-old, watching the food network, eyes glued to the screen as we entered the lobby of our apartment building. I glanced quickly over at the mailboxes afraid of what I would see. Sure enough, along with the bills was the fancy letter that I'd been dreading. It seemed as if everything was silent as I took it from the mailbox. I realized that it was addressed to the parents of Bailey Jemison, and I tried to respond to Bailey's questions as we walked up the stairs, but it was very hard. When we reached our apartment, I unlocked the door, my fingers still trembling.

"And then, Aaron stole my Barbie cowgirl and-" Bailey said. "Bryn! Are you even listening?"

"Yeah, sure. Aaron stole Barbie cowgirl," I recited. "Let's start dinner."

As I opened the pantry door, the phone rang. It was Mrs. Crantree, Bailey's principal.

"Hello! Is Mrs. Jemison available?" she croaked in her high pitched voice.

"Not at the moment," I said. "But, I can I take a message."

She paused, "No, no! That's okay, but could you just tell her to call me back at her earliest convenience?"

"Okay."

"Thank you," she said, and we hung up.

"Bryn?" Bailey asked. "Are you okay?"

I quickly turned off my worried expression and answered, "I'm fine. Let's make dinner."

As it turned out, to keep Bailey from asking questions, we had rice and broccoli. When we were nearly finished, Mom stormed in, dark bags still under her eyes. As soon as she came in, she sat down on our old and tattered sofa

"Hi, Mommy!" Bailey shouted. "I made something for you."

Before Mom could comment, Bailey was in the process of running to her book bag. She pulled out a yellow card with a picture on it.

When Mom opened it, she smiled at the hand-drawn picture of her and Bailey with the words 'I Love You' written on the bottom.

"Do you like it, Mommy?" Bailey asked.

"Oh, Honey. I love it!" Mom exclaimed, scooping her up for a hug. Bailey beamed.

* * *

After dinner Bailey colored in her Dora coloring book while I did the dishes.

"Bails, Hon, go to your room for a sec. Put on your pajamas and I'll tuck you in, in a minute. As soon as Bailey was out of earshot, Mom began.

"Mrs. Crantree called me today saying that due to inconsistent payments, Bailey is forbidden to go back to her school."

"Oh, Mom! I'm so..."

"Come 'ere," she said.

I lay in her lap and she said, "All I wanted to do in my lifetime was to let you both have the joy of education. Your dad won't help me pay for anything, and because I've been too dependent on the government, they won't assist me anymore. I don't have any money!" She started to cry.

"Mom, don't cry," I said.

"And I told that Mrs. Crantree some words that I truly regret…about discrimination. I mean, she didn't even *try* to help me!"

"Oh, sorry, I forgot to tell you she called today," I said, suddenly regretting it.

"Oh, I don't need people like her anyway," she said, swatting her hand in the air. She swallowed hard and wiped her eyes using her sleeve. "I need help."

I reached over and grabbed a tissue from a nearby box. "Here," I said giving it to her.

"Thanks," she said. I put my head down in defeat. When she saw this she quickly said, "Well enough of this. We've been here before. We'll manage. Go to sleep."

"Okay," I said, giving her a big, long hug and taking in her wonderful, motherly scent. Heading to Bailey's room, she turned to me and said, "*I love you Bryn*, goodnight."

* * *

Mom leaves for her nursing shift at the Lincoln Memorial Hospital at 5:00 in the morning, silently, leaving the trace of a heavenly coffee aroma behind. That's why when I heard a knock on the door around 6:00, I couldn't imagine why. Still in an early morning haze, I looked through the peephole to see two police officers standing in front of me. Slowly, I opened the door.

"Hello," one officer with a weird haircut and a beard said. "Are you Bryn Jemison?"

"Uh, yes," I answered, mid yawn. "Excuse me. Please come in."

Both officers came in with a very unsettling look on their faces.

"How can I help you?"

"The question is, Sweetheart, how can *we* help *you*?" the ordinary looking man said.

"Excuse me?"

"I'm extremely sorry, but your mother, Brandy Jemison, d-died in an automobile accident this morning."

To tell the absolute truth, I don't remember a thing that occurred after hearing the horrific news. All I can remember doing is running, crying, thinking, and screaming. That's the thing about life. You say that you are going to do 'such and such' when whatever happens, but realistically, you'll never know until it does indeed happen. All I can do right now is run, cry, and scream.

* * *

After the funeral, I loaded Aunt Cecelia's car. I took what few belongings that we had left along with a family portrait that hung in the family room. Because Bailey didn't have a car seat, I had to put down pillows for her to sit on. With her small, old Barbie suitcases in hand, Bailey took one last painful look at the naked, lonely walls that surrounded us. While looking around, I just happened to gaze at my mother's favorite fake rose, imbedded in a short white vase. Since she was a woman who absolutely dreaded death, it was always easier for her to look at this fake rose rather that a real one, because she knew that one day a real rose would die. Since this one always gave her much joy when needed, I decided that it was only right to take it with me. I would always have it as a memento of her to honor her interminable appreciation of life.

"Come on! Jesus! I don't have all day!" Aunt Cecelia barked, killing my memory instantly.

"We're coming!" I yelled back.

"Bryn, do we *have* to live with Aunt Cecelia?" Bailey asked.

"Yes, if you don't want to live on the street," I said.

"Well, why can't we stay here?" she pouted.

"Come on. We'll have fun!"

"Sure," she muttered.

"If you girls don't get your butts down here right now-"

"I can't promise, Bails, but I'll do my best," I said looking at the rose. "I'll try."

Remembering Aunt Cecelia, I quickly led Bailey into the hallway and locked up. Slowly, we walked down the stairs. Once we met up with Aunt Cecelia, she instructed us to get in the car, but it was locked.

"Get in right now," she commanded.

"I can't," I said. "The door is locked."

"Don't you sass me, little girl!" she bellowed. "I don't have to do this at all, you know! Now get your little ungrateful butts in the car!" All in one move, she unlocked the car door and shot me the evil look that I sensed meant 'you might want to shut your mouth and get in the car.'

"Bryn!" she spat.

"But Brynee, I'm scared! And I want Mommy!" Bailey started to silently cry. All I could do was pat her on the back and lead her into the car.

When we finally were settled in, Aunt Cecelia looked me in the eye. "It's about time, Girl! I can't wait to get out of this dilapidated dump!"

I rolled my eyes and sighed a heavy sigh.

"Don't you sigh at me! I surely do not have to help you."

Now my adrenaline was really pumping. I felt like my veins would pop out at any second! You'd think she would actually feel bad for us.

"You know what, Aunt Cecelia," I started.

"You let me talk! You can talk when I'm done!" she barked. She pointed her finger in my face, and Bailey winced. "Now, I'm doing this out of my husband's cousin's memory! So, don't you sigh, talk, or interrupt me. In fact, don't even *breathe*!"

Bailey's eyes suddenly grew wider as we looked at each other; we were shocked.

"I don't like this situation as it is," Aunt Cecelia started again. "So, you two better get yourselves together, and do it quickly. Do you both understand me?"

I nodded slightly and secretly rolled my eyes.

"All right now!" she said, fixing her expensive purple suit and checking her tight messy bun in the rearview mirror. For an insane lady, she surely dressed nicely. She wore a lot of makeup in an attempt to hide the fact that she was only 46, but looked much older.

Unlike any other family member I knew, she was the only one that had big bucks. I'm talking ridiculous homes in other countries. Her offspring and generations to come were all sure to inherit millions! Apparently, she inherited all of her money and book smarts from her father, Pete Hariz Lopez, a famous scholar who received the Noble Peace Prize for his inspirational book. Aunt Cecelia Maria Lopez was set to follow in her father's footsteps with two bestsellers of her own. Still, with all the money she had, she was so bitter. Well, it didn't matter what caused the old, sorry, sour, boring woman to go crazy; all that mattered was figuring out how to stay on her good side…without puking!

"So, Aunt Cecelia," I said, trying to break the silence. "I hear you have two bestsellers. The most recent book was on the *New York Times* Best Sellers' list. What caused you to write such an exquisite and motivating novel?"

"It's not a novel!" she snapped. "And my business is mine and mine only!"

"Sorry! I was just trying to break the awkward silen-"

"Excuse me! My name is on my book as the author. Is yours?"

"No."

"Then shut your mouth!"

"Aunt Cecelia," Bailey said, cautiously. "Can you please turn up the radio?"

"Little girl! Do you really desire to listen to that rubbish on the radio?"

"What's rubbish, Aunt Cecelia?"

"Rubbish, Child, if you must know, is that garbage that plays on the radio constantly. God, that stuff gives me migraines!"

"Sorry I asked," Bailey mumbled.

"Aunt Cecelia, there are a few jazz stations to listen to," I commented, delighted to start a happier conversation.

"Those stations remind me of too much grief, pain, and suffering, though. After awhile, it can make you crazy!"

"I understand," I said, as we pulled up to a fancy iron gate.

"Corinne Marie Lopez," Aunt Cecelia spoke into a matching iron box. "Five, sixteen, zero, three," she also said. I guessed it was someone's person's birthday.

"Access granted," the little box spoke back.

We traveled about a quarter of a mile when we came up to another iron box with green buttons with another iron gate past it. Aunt Cecelia put her hand on it and it lit up.

"Access granted," the second box spoke. Finally, we reached a hill after traveling another quarter of a mile. Man, she must have been extremely wealthy to have so many security gates.

The house was massive; it was a four story brick house completed with a gray stoned addition attached to the garage. Far in the distance there was what appeared to be a cottage with smoke coming from the chimney. I was guessing that it was another rancher house. I bet she could fit about seven families in it and still have plenty of room for Bailey, herself, and me! I couldn't believe it. She was like my Oprah. Where had this family been all of my life? I instantly felt like an ant at Six Flags! I'd also never forget the "L" shaped bush sculpture that was placed on the front lawn.

"Wow, Aunt Cecelia! This is a very pretty house. It looks like my Barbie Dream house only bigger!" Bailey shouted.

"Thank you," Aunt Cecelia whispered. "Your bags are in the trunk, and Felix is off for today, so I hope you two have been doing your pushups! I'd like to help and chat, but I need coffee now," she said, while walking into the house leaving Bailey and me to get our bags and lug them up the Lincoln-Memorial-like steps ourselves.

Bailey struggled with her Barbie suitcases and a matching carry-on bag, while I tried to lift two large blue suitcases and two carry-ons containing more of Bailey's things, when I noticed something. This house contained nine bedrooms and six and a half bathrooms, but Aunt Cecelia was single. Aunt Cecelia was not a social woman, yet she had dozens of pictures framed everywhere and a looping digital picture frame on the mantle. I noticed that she had many pictures of a little girl with long black hair. I've seen some of those before in my mother's album, but never knew who it was. Well, whoever she was, she seemed *happy*, so how could she be related to Aunt Cecelia?

* * *

"Bryn, this is your new room," Aunt Cecelia said while ushering me into the room of my dreams. It was like walking into a fairytale. The ceiling favored a cathedral building with its very high arch. There were steps leading up to a platform that contained a king-sized bed and, best of all, at the click of a button, a plasma TV came down from the ceiling at the foot of the bed! There were many windows to let in the sunlight warming the cream walls, and chocolate brown silk bedspread trimmed with cream lace. This room was a huge step up from my previous room that I shared with Bailey, where I had encountered numerous rats at night.

"Oh, Aunt Cecelia!" I exclaimed, taking it all in. "Thank you so much!" For the first time since I had seen her all day she was smiling.

"I hope this room fits your likings."

"Of course!" I was beaming.

"Aunt Cecelia?" Bailey asked. "Can we unpack now?"

"In here?" she asked while peering over her glasses.

"If Bryn gets the floor, then I can get the bed, right?"

"No!"

"Well should we share the bed, then?" Bailey asked.

"No, no, no, child! There's plenty of rooms in the house for everyone!" Aunt Cecelia chuckled. Why was she still smiling? Was she on drugs?

"You mean, I get my very own room?" Bailey squealed.

"Your room is positioned so that if you get scared at night, you can walk through your closet and get into your sister's room."

"You really mean it?" Bails asked.

"Well, yes!"

Before she could say another word, Bailey ran full speed towards her, hugging her knees. For a second, Aunt Cecelia just stood there, not responding to Bailey; then she warmed up a bit, smiled, and returned the hug.

* * *

It's been four days since the big move of terror. I had to sit through six sessions already of lectures explaining discipline, rules, and plain old annoying reminders of the favor she was supposedly 'lending' us. That woman was surely even sourer than a lemon. Well, at least Bailey was protected and content; that's all I really could ever want.

For dinner, we had coq co van with a citrus salad prepared by her personal chef Loi Vandallas. Like every new meal, it was the best thing I ever had tasted. Basking in the ambiance, I nearly choked when talk of school came up. Aunt Cecelia said I would soon be attending Myra Dayvasse's School for Young Women. I was not happy at all.

"Bryn Amelia, I know this a big step up for you now, at this time, but it'll be worth it. You'd have to start another school, anyway. You may as well get the first day over with ASAP. MDSYW is the best school you'll ever attend anyway," she said.

"What are you trying to say?' I asked her "That I'm not smart enough to make it into college? Is that it?"

"Well," she said, stopping to take a sip of her wine, "to tell you the complete truth, because that's what you want to hear, right? Anyway, truth is you're not bright. You're not pretty. So basically you have no chance in today's world." She shrugged her shoulders.

"I can't believe as my family you would say that to me! But wait I can because you're the devil!"

"Bryn Amelia Jemison!" she said in disbelief.

I threw my cloth napkin at her glass of red wine causing it to spill on her white table cloth and ran upstairs.

* * *

I spent all night waiting for Aunt Cecelia to come and to talk to me. Not surprisingly, only Bailey came upstairs to comfort me by singing *Tomorrow* from the movie *Annie*. After I sent her to bed, I got to think, "It'd be much easier to raise Bailey back at home than it would be to deal with Aunt Cecelia until *she died*!" Even though it was pouring rain, according to the weatherman, it would stop around 2:30 A.M. I had two hours before it would start up again. Still, I thought it was enough time to flag a cab and get back home in time! It was definitely worth a shot!

While I was quietly packing, I heard Bailey scream. Quickly, I dropped my toiletries, and ran across the hallway. Bailey was hiding under her green covers and crying. As I sat on her bed and pulled back the covers, she started screaming my name.

"Bryn! Brynee I'm scared! I wanna go home!" Bailey said over the loud thunder.

All of a sudden a big streak of lightning permeated the black sky, and she started screaming again.

"Shhhh!" I whispered firmly. Then I began to sing her favorite song, *Tomorrow*.

Bailey yawned and said, "I Love you, Bryn" before dozing off.

"I love you, too," I whispered. I lay my head on the other pillow and fell asleep.

* * *

"Boom! Boom! Wooosh!" I awoke to the sound of thunder, and what do you know; it was already 2:13 A.M. Remembering my plans, I found Bailey's suitcases in her closet and began to empty out her drawers. After packing her dolls, I checked the room one last time to make sure I didn't leave anything behind. I woke Bailey up and told her the plan. Many whispered questions later, we arranged how we would carry our luggage. I told Bailey that she was strictly to remain silent until we left the driveway; we made sure not to roll our luggage, and we carried it instead. It was easy to sneak into the kitchen because Aunt Cecelia's bedroom was in the opposite wing of the house; what a relief! I ordered Bailey to grab six TV Dinners out of the freezer. I grabbed some crackers, cans of soup, cans of vegetables and fruits, and little snacks for us to eat back at home. I figured in order to last maybe a week or two we needed food until I got a job. I quickly bagged the items, adding water bottles and Hi-C fruit punch pouches.

All of a sudden, I heard the wooden floor creak several times upstairs. Briskly, I turned off all of the many kitchen lights, and

Bailey and I hid behind the central island. Aunt Cecelia came halfway downstairs in her fuzzy yellow slippers, a matching robe, and a green tea mask hiding her facial features. From the glass kitchen table I could see her look back and forth from the table to the island. I saw she was looking in my direction. I noticed my foot was peeking out a bit, so I jerked it back.

Finally satisfied, she gave up and went back upstairs. Bailey and I simultaneously sighed, then walked to the backdoor, which wasn't alarmed. While arriving outside, the storm greeted us.

"Are you sure we should leave?" Bailey asked, already soaked.

"Come on," I said, ignoring her question. "Put your raincoat on."

"But…"

"Now!"

"Boom! Whoosh! Boom! Boom!" The thunder roared. The lightning followed, lighting up the sky. We continued to walk without looking back.

* * *

The first break that we encountered was the first bus stop, which was three and a half

miles away. It would take us downtown. Of course, there was no roof on the bus stop

stand, but just a plain wooden bench! Bailey and I sat on the wooden bench, getting soaked,

waiting for the bus that was due to arrive any second now. A half an hour later, I walked

looking for help or a sign from heaven, *something*.

In the distance I spotted a white sign taped to a nearby pole, saying, 'Due to the extreme, inconvenient weather, the Georgia Bus Line won't be making any stops.'

Oh, come on.

I turned to look at Bailey, and I noticed that she was crying.

"Let's take a break," I said.

"Here?" she asked

"Uhhhh…" I looked around. There had to be somewhere we could go! My heart

was pounding through my chest, and a tight knot was forming in the back of my throat. I

looked around and realized that we were at the wrong bus station. We had gone the

wrong way.

This is just perfect, I thought. This part of Georgia was deserted! No Burger

King. No Wawa. Not even a gas station for miles! Wait a minute. "A gas station!" I

shouted. Bailey just shook her head. I was obviously going nuts, since the words 'bucket'

or 'circus' were just as random as 'gas station' to her. I collected our belongings.

"Bryn. We just sat down! Let's just take a break, please!"

"In the rain?"

I didn't wait for an answer back, took her hand and started walking with purpose.

We walked and walked for what seemed like hours. Bailey complained, but I still hadn't

lost all hope, yet. Minutes later, I saw light; it was just a speckle, but just enough to

regain my confidence.

"A light!" Bailey shrieked. "It's really a light!" She ran to the light as fast as she

Could, ignoring my constant calls to come back.

Honestly, I felt horrible! Bailey was running towards the light as if it was her only

hope left of living. But my instincts told me she certainly wouldn't be the only one! I ran

as fast as I could, and sure enough, we reached a Shell gas station. I could instantly hear

the 'Hallelujah' chorus in my head as I secured my surroundings.

"Bryn! Can we stop here? I need to use the bathroom." Bailey asked. At this rate, knowing where we were, I wasn't ready to stop, but seeing Bailey's pitiful, longing face, made me agree to it.

"Ok. We'll stop here, for now, but you'll have to be quick."

"Oh, thank-you!" she said dramatically, and breathed a sigh of relief.

I pushed the glass door open cautiously and heard a door chime. A dark-skinned heavyset man

sitting at the register shot us a look, as though puncturing a hole through my face.

"Hi," I said nervously to cut the tension. I grabbed Bailey's hand and walked

into aisle 4.

"Bailey. We're only going to be in here for a minute. I see a sign for the restroom back

there." I pointed to a sign in the back of the store. "Come on." When we walked into the next

aisle, two other older men looked me up and down suspiciously.

"Hurry up," I whispered to Bailey who decided to bend down and tie her shoe on the way

to the restroom.

About three minutes later, as we were making a dash out the store to avoid the man's

glare, he started to talk to Bailey.

" Hey! You Celie's kid?" he said to Bailey. "I've seen you around here. I think.

Word of advice… run away!"

"Fred! That ain't Celie's kid. Her kid died of cancer in April!"

"Yeah." Fred said. "Was wonder'n why there were two."

"Her child *died* ?" I asked in disbelief.

"Yeah!" another man said. "Where have you been?! Cecelia's been acting like a

mad woman ever since!"

"Not to mention her miscarriage afterwards." Fred said.

"What?" I had to hold onto the magazine stand to balance.

"Yeah, child! Celie hardly speaks now. The nasty ol' hag!" The other man spoke.

＊ ＊ ＊

For about what seemed forever, Bailey and I walked without speaking.

Remembering what my mom used to say, I decided to be the 'bigger person.'

"Bailey, I'm really sorry. I destroyed the one chance we ever had to settle in and get a good education. I'm ashamed…"

"Wait, Bryn! Aunt Cecelia's car!" Sure enough her BMW came rolling up in front of us.

"We are too much for her, though. It's better to be respectful and stay away," I said, doubting that she would welcome us back with open arms.

"Bryn!" she said yanking my arm towards the car. "Are you stupid or something?"

I ignored her and started walking alone. Six paces later she finally gave up and saw it my way.

It was too late. Aunt Cecelia pulled up next to Bailey. Seeing her worried, red eyes knocked the wind out of me.

"Dear God!" She choked getting out of the car. "Get in the car right this minute!"

"Aunt Cecelia," I interrupted, "I would like to respect your wishes. I would like to raise Bailey back where she and I both belong," She watched me for a moment.

"If you'd really like to respect my wishes," she said, "you'd get in the car."

* * *

As soon as we got back to the mansion, I was told to tuck Bailey in and report downstairs. After doing just that, I was ushered into her grand library.

"Have a seat," she said, gesturing me to an expensive red velvet chair. She did one of her classic stares into my eyes, and I wished that I could just melt away.

"Bryn… I have to be frank with you. You must know the truth." She took a deep breath and sipped her tea.

"Your relative, Corrine Marie, my first and, regretfully, only daughter was born on May 16th, 2003. It was the best day of my life. The weather was perfect and nothing could bring me down." She smiled. "As I expected, she warmed my heart with her

72

beautiful smile. Oh, how I adored my little Cory! My husband would just walk into her room during the night and watch her sleep. We both thanked God for our wonderful daughter. Her father and I always imagined that the future ahead would be worry free. She was mine forever, or so I thought. It turned out that she'd inherited my father's smarts. When she was five, I realized that her school's work was not at all challenging enough for her. I mean, who learns their ABC's *every day* in kindergarten! In fact, she often complained it was too easy, and annoyingly boring. She would beg me to teach her more, and insisted that I start my own school. I knew the people. I certainly had the money, and my number one fan, Corrine.

Everything was set; I had bought books, supplies, and a nearby building that was once a boutique. Things were really changing for the better!" She took another sip of her tea. "But, that all stopped a month later when I found out that I was pregnant again! I was ecstatic," she said through tears. "Sometimes, I'd even wake up to find Corinne in my bed rubbing my stomach! Those were the about good times." She sighed, moaned, then took a picture of a little girl off her desk and held it to her heart. "Soon after, I had learned that Corinne had kidney cancer. She'd been living with it for a while. I never noticed any symptoms…. and then… just one day it decided….to show its ugly face. After months and months of medication, the doctor said it was useless. She would soon… die.

"The next week, I had her stay home from school. We went to baseball games, the movies, and I planned a trip for Disney. This picture was taken at the big game!" She handed me another picture of a little tan girl with a plaid skirt and a pink tank top giving a thumbs up sign to the camera. Aunt Cecelia was right!

She was adorable. The next night we packed our bags. She was so excited." She grinned, then frowned. "But the next day… she didn't wake up."

"I'm… sorry," I said, because I had no idea what else to say.

"I was so stressed that I had a miscarriage. My husband said that he was sorry, but we didn't have anything left in our relationship without Corinne, and just … walked.

And here I am now with two wonderful girls that God has just given to me, and I can't even embrace that! Corinne used to say I had the power of giving happiness. Well, not anymore! Please, I know I'm not the best at being a guardian, but please… forgive me. Please." She started sobbing uncontrollably.

I ran to her and hugged her and said, "Corinne, would want you to be happy. Don't cry. You will make your dream come true. For Corinne… you will."

Dear Diary,

Today we cut the ribbon to the Corinne Elementary School of Love. Can you believe it? Aunt Cecelia has her own new school, which is supported by her two new number-one fans, Bails and me. All advanced kids in the township attend to enjoy great educational experiences. The school is a big part of the community. Other people have donated supplies, and computers. There are smart boards in all 19 class rooms, plus a nursery, and a preschool. To make this happen, I had to forgive Aunt Cecelia. God put it in my heart to forgive her and showed me that He truly can make a way out of no way!

Aunt Cecelia even got an award from the mayor for her efforts! Even Bailey is now officially moved into the house into Corinne's huge room. From 46 Barbie dolls to a queen sized pink silk covered bed, Bails got it all! And me, I got the gift of volunteering. Twice a week, I go to the school and read books and play with the preschoolers. But I have to say, the best part was forgiving Aunt Cecelia. For me, Bailey, and Aunt Cecelia, forgiveness was the best gift that God could've ever given to us. I still miss my mom, but I know she's in a better place. At least, I have the gift of love and her beautiful rose. I will never forget her, and I thank her for raising me well. Gotta go, big-sister-homework-helper duty calls!

I Am Forgiving: *Forbearing one another, and forgiving one another, if any man have a quarrel against any: even as Christ forgave you, so also do ye.*

- Colossians 3:13

I Am Amiable

"Okay, pencils down," Mrs. Geoffrey said. "You have just completed section two of the language section of the Colorado Student Assessment Program 11 test or CSAP for short. Now we will stop and take a five-minute break. Stay in your seats. You may talk quietly. Gina Keagan and Mia Miller, come with me,"

I quickly got to my feet and followed Mrs. Geoffrey along with Gina to the back of the classroom. The pressure was off for me, because there was no way that I could've been in trouble. Teachers adored me, because of my squeaky-clean image and spectacular grades.

"One of you is in serious trouble!" she started.

Gina gave me an evil glare.

We both knew that those words meant Gina had done something wrong. From first grade through fifth we were best friends until one day, in fifth grade. I noticed that Gina was peering over at my test papers. Gina wasn't exactly discreet about it. In fact she specifically peered down at my papers, not caring enough to hide this misdeed. Gina always thought that I didn't mind, because we were best friends. She continued to cheat on every test day after day. I always wanted to speak up, but she threatened that if I told, she would tell everyone my deepest, darkest secret that I'd shared with her in fourth grade.

"Oh, you'll feel better once you give me the answers. That's what friends do!" Gina would tell me when I threatened to tell on her. I busted her in sixth grade when she cheated on the CSAP. Of course, she denied it. She made our sixth grade homeroom teacher, Mr. Osborne, think that I cheated. With her convincing story and her friends vouching for her, it was easy enough for Mr. Osborne to believe the lie. I spent a week at home on suspension and almost received an incomplete on my test. But my dad, an esteemed attorney, got me out of it. Since then, Gina told everyone in school that I couldn't be trusted, because I supposedly cheated off of everyone's paper. My father was infuriated by the false accusations and attacks on my reputation. I don't know how, but he managed to use the school's camera to prove that I was innocent. Gina received a big fat zero on the test that year, and I was given a retest and aced it. From then on, Gina was always in the hot seat and closely watched. She was angry at me and the world, but I didn't care, as long as she was seated away from me and could no longer take credit for my work.

"Gina, when Mr. Benson took over for me about 20 minutes ago, I happened to be looking at the camera in the classroom. I saw someone who looked just like you looking over at Mia's test," Mrs. Geoffrey said. "You know how much trouble you're in?"

Gina stared blankly, but her facial expression said it all. She was thinking, 'I'm caught again!'

"Mia, did you know about this?" my teacher questioned.

"No!" I replied. Why would *I*, of all people, let Gina cheat off of me again?

"Ms. Keagan, you are in serious trouble! Go to Mr. Milliano's office! He'll go into further detail about your punishments." Mrs. Geoffrey's voice showed no sign of sympathy for Gina. "Now, I have to write a letter to the state. I'm afraid you will get another zero, and we'll have to call your parents! Do you realize how long the process will be to cancel your scores? I assure you Ms, Keagan, the process is very painstaking. You'll probably get suspended as well."

"No! Don't call my mom. She'll go crazy! Please! I only cheated because I didn't know most of the answers! It was the only way-"

"Ms. Keagan, you can't talk your way out of this one! Not this time. "Go down and see Mr. Milliano this instant!" Gina dropped her head and walked slowly out the door.

Mrs. Geoffrey instructed me to sit back down, as we all started section three of the CSAP.

* * *

After testing that day, I went to Mrs. Geoffrey's desk.

"Mrs. Geoffrey, Gina has been through a lot, but…," I paused. Did I really want to say this?

"Go on," Mrs. Geoffrey encouraged.

"Ever since I can remember, Gina has cheated off of me. She said that I was being a real friend. You probably know this already, but in sixth grade, Gina cheated off of my standardized tests. She's a very imprudent 17 year-old!" I protested. "You'd think that she'd stop cheating! It's just that… We need to be separated. Can you please talk to Mr. Milliano about changing the three classes that we have together? This second semester I want to focus on improving my academic career and I can't do that if I am suspected of cheating. I never would cheat off anyone. It would be a disgrace to the art of academics. As you know, I have been accepted into the National Honor Society and this sort of accusation could-"

"Brinnnng!" the bell rang for next period.

"Come back after lunch. I want to hear more about this," Mrs. Geoffrey said.

"Okay," I said. "Thanks for your time."

"Yes, of course! In the meantime I'll see what I can do."

* * *

"Oh! Imprudent am I?" Gina asked.

Poor girl, she probably had no idea what the word 'imprudent' meant. I slammed my locker shut and started to walk away. She quickly kept up with my fast pace. I went to turn the corner and she blocked my path.

"What are you talking about?" I asked nervously.

"News travels quick, Mia!"

"So?"

"Don't think I don't know about your little chat with Geoffrey!"

"What?"

"Look, my patience is wearing thin. You better get yourself together. See, the way I see it, you are messin' with my future. That's not okay!"

"So? What are you saying?"

"I'm sayin', watch your back! If you're lucky, I won't beat the snot out of you, and you'll live to see next year!" She jumped in my face. I flinched. "Now what?"

"Ms. Keagan," Mr. Jones interrupted. "Get to class!" Gina ran into the west wing.

"Thanks." I said to him.

I had to watch my back. Lord knows what Gina would do to me.

* * *

"You've got mail!" my computer chirped. I ran over to it, eager to hear from my dad who was in New York trying to solve an important case.

From: Daringdanny@yahoo.com.
To: Mamamia21@gmail.com.

Hey M,
    Jenny's throwing a party on Saturday at the skating center. Don't worry. Keagan won't be there. Attached is all the info jenny sent me about it. Forward this to Em, Alyssa, Miles, Casey, Jill, Dylan, and Autumn! C u there…

Danny

It was just my friend, Danielle. There was going to be a party?

From: Mamamia21@gmail.com.
To: Daringdanny@yahoo.com.

RU sure Krazy Keagan won't B there?

From: Daringdanny@yahoo.com
To: Mamamia21@gmail.com.

(I know you hate your first name), but, *Alexis* Mia, would I lie 2 U? ☺

From: Mamamia21@gmail.com.
To: Daringdanny@yahoo.com

Let me think, yes! (and don't call me Alexis; it's annoying! ☺)

From: Daringdanny@yahoo.com.
To: Mamamia21@gmail.com.

Good answer! C U there.

From: Mamamia21@gmail.com.
To: Daringdanny@yahoo.com.

Don't bet on it! Did I actually say I'm going??

From: Daringdanny@yahoo.com.
To: Mamamia21@gmail.com.

Puh-leaze! Spare me the excuses!

From: Mamamia21@gmail.com.
To: Daringdanny@yahoo.com.

OK. Pick me up at 8!

From: Daringdanny@yahoo.com.
To: Mamamia21@gmail.com.

Don't count on it ☺

I smiled. As long as Keagan didn't show up, maybe a party wouldn't be too terrible.

* * *

On Saturday I spent forever trying to find a cute outfit. By 7:30 I found a vintage dark green sweater dress and black leggings with black stilettos. I finished getting dressed just in time to straighten my medium length blond hair.

At 8 o'clock, I finished applying lip gloss just as the doorbell rang. I stuck silver hoops into my ears, my contacts into my eyes and raced to the door. On my way out, I grabbed my clutch.

"Bye, Mom!" I shouted. "Be back at 10. I'm with Danny at the Marion Township Skating Rink! Love you."

I ran out to Danny's car to find Alyssa inside. As soon as I opened the car door, Zedd's *Clarity* blasted from the speakers.

"Why are you my clarity," we all sang as Danny sped off in her blue Chevy. I put my window down and let the wind blow through my hair. I could tell that the night was going to be great!

* * *

"Hey! Hey!" shouted Jenny as we walked in. She had to scream over *Slow Down* by Selena Gomez blasting from the rink's speakers.

"The rink's ours for the night! You can skate on the rink in the second room, dance, talk, play flag football with the guys in that room. Ew," She paused dramatically. "Or, get your nails done at that station over there." Sure enough Milan's Salon was doing nails in the corner of the room. "Food's downstairs and the D.J's over there!" She pointed to a college boy mixing music on a turntable while taking requests from a line of girls.

"Fresh from college!" She eyed the DJ. "Anyway, have fun!" She ran to join Megan and Sean on the rink.

* * *

After hours and hours of what seemed like years of fun and dancing, I had to sit down. Danny went to get some pizza, and I watched the people on the rink during the 'couples only' song. Danielle came back with a delightfully sized slice of pizza. I was getting ready to take my first bite when *Baby Got Back* started playing. The strobe lights started flashing. I couldn't resist! Danny, Casey, and I headed straight to the dance floor in the other room.

"You get sprung!" Everyone shouted. Everyone around me was dancing to the beat. I was dancing with Danny, when I spotted Gina's body sliding down the wall on the far end of the room. Wasn't she not supposed to be at the party? She looked so scary under the black lights of the room. I skated over to her to get a closer look; she had slipped in her skates and fainted. I saw that there were red bloodstains all over her clothes. In disbelief, I found Megan sitting down.

"Megan, where's Jenny?"

"I think I saw her in the bathroom a minute ago," she replied.

"Thanks." I ran down another hall and into the bathroom.

"Jenny!" I called as I searched. "Jenny!" No one replied.

On my way out of the bathroom, I saw girls in a corner injecting a needle in their arms. They, too, had blood stains all over their clothes. On the other side of the bathroom, I saw girls from my grade smoking. They looked washed out and very weak. It did not take long for me to realize what was really happening. I knew that I should leave. Usually in movies I've seen, this would be the part when the cops decided to show up. I had to leave! As soon as I exhaled after leaving the bathroom, I called Danny on her phone and tried to tell her what I had just seen. My phone had limited reception, so I had to walk around the corner and back to the dance floor. I was racing to my friends when I heard someone shout, "Freeze!"

I froze and found a cop in front of me. "I got a call that some kids have been using drugs and drinking alcohol." He addressed the crowd boldly.

"I want to know who has been using them and who supplied it. Make a horizontal line so we can check you all out," said the same intimidating officer. "And don't even think about leaving the premises. We have you all surrounded!" I head a few people groaning.

Everyone formed a line. Three cops started checking out the line of startled teens. They each held up a breath test and checked our eyes with flashlights.

After about twenty minutes of checking pupils and searching handbags the police took 9 girls and 12 guys to their patrol cars. One remained frozen under the watch of the tallest officer. He arrested Gina and took her to the side, but I could still hear him talking. He told her that she had the right to remain silent and stated her rights while leading her to his patrol car.

As she was taken away, I thought about our old friendship, our old secrets, our old trust in each other and loyalty. She was never like this…ever. This couldn't be her! Not that girl that dreamed that she would be a lawyer? Not the girl who used to believe in herself!

"Yeah I got 'em. Yes, boss, don't worry," said a cop with a deep voice. Soon Gina slumped helplessly in the patrol car while everyone watched in amazement. I had to do something. Without thinking, I quickly flagged down a cab to get to the police station.

By the time I walked in the door, Gina was already using the phone. Her mom's voice was so loud and intense that I thought I felt the ground shaking.

"You did what?"

"Mom, I'm sorry! Please pay my bail. I'll do anything! Please just one more time," Gina pleaded.

"No!" the voice bellowed. "This is the fifth time this year that I'm paying some fine for your foolish mistakes!" Gina started to cry, making her mascara run down her cheeks. "*You* better pay your own bail, or you can rot in jail for all I care! Make your decision. Good-bye!"

I watched a cop lead Gina away. She was sobbing. I couldn't stand to see her that way. Maybe I could help. I had about $300 of birthday money and from babysitting money, about $120. I had saved for a while. Surely it was enough to help an old friend.

"I'm here to see Gina Keagan," I told the guard who led me to a big room with bare white walls.

"Wait right here," the guard said.

Five minutes later, he led me into a booth and Gina was sitting on the opposite side of a glass barrier. The second guard told me that I had to use the phone to talk to her. When she answered her voice was so low that she sounded like a little kid.

"Gina." I said calmly. "I know you feel like you don't need any help, but I am here for you. I have $420 saved. You can have it all. Just trust me. I believe that you can turn your life around. We're going to get you out of here."

"Go away!" She screamed to the top of her lungs. I paused.

"Listen," I said. "I know you feel abandoned and hurt, and you probably don't want to see anyone now. I know we are no longer friends, but deep inside I know you would do it for me. I don't think that you deserve to be here. I can remember the time when you supported me after my grandfather died. You really had my back, and I will never forget that. But, you have changed. Our friendship ended a long time ago when you lost sight of what really mattered. "

"You sound like my mom," she said with her head hung low. "Actually," she added, slightly lifting her head, "you don't, because normally she's screaming!"

"I want to bail you out. You can change. I know you can. It's not too late." I sighed. "Just let me take care of this now, and then we can go back to hating each other," I said to lighten the mood.

"No!" Gina sobbed. "You've been too kind to me. I always took advantage of your help. I don't deserve this. You have helped enough. Right now, I have to suffer. It's time I accepted responsibility without hurting the ones I love." She stopped to blow her nose.

"Gina"

"No! You don't have to help me! I blew it. After graduation I'm gonna be working some dead end job, and I'm gonna be homeless!" She paused. "I'm never gonna be somebody! I'm nobody."

"No!" I said. "You can be somebody. It all starts with believing in yourself! Just believe, because you are so much better than this. I have seen you do really great things. The first step is to get saved and start going to church, maybe get some counseling." I could tell that I was starting to lose her interest because she was staring in another direction.

"You're being so nice. What have I ever done that was right when we were friends?"

"We stopped being friends?" I smiled. Gina did too.

"I mean, even now. The way you are treating me now."

I smiled.

"Like that," she continued. "God will bless you. You just stay on the right track with school. You'll be a doctor for sure!"

"Maybe, but I want to help you. I just feel that you can make it. Something just tells me that I have to do this."

"I'll have to start all over," she said.

"Yeah, but it doesn't have to be so bad. You can retake up courses to catch up. It doesn't have to be that hard. You'll be back on track in no time."

"You think so?"

"I'm serious."

"No one has ever done anything like this for me before." she said.

"Now let me get my money."

"You're the best!" Gina said.

I pointed to God.

"He's in me!" I replied. Then, I hurried out of the police station.

* * *

It was just my luck that it started to rain; let me correct that, pour. So, unfortunately, the cab driver took forever and a day just to reach my house. When I arrived home, I gave my mom a brief summary of the chaotic scene at the party.

"Are you sure you want to use your money on some friend that betrayed you more than you'll ever know?" Mom asked in amazement.

"It's the right thing to do." I sighed. "And if I don't get her out soon…" I stopped and shuddered. "I've been praying to God, and he is telling me that I should help her. I am just doing what He set out for me to do." With my last remark, I walked past my silent mother, and out my front door.

* * *

As soon as the cab stopped, I paid the driver and ran into the police station.

When I entered, I ran into an unpleasant surprise. Gina was with her nasty, evil witch of a mother.

"I ought to beat the freaking mess out of you! You are not going to be happy tonight," she bellowed in Gina's face before handing uneven piles of small bills of money to a secretary. "You better be happy I brought my $530! But thanks to you, your brothers and sisters will be eating slop in the dark!"

By this point, Gina was hunched over on a nearby bench shaking and crying. "Mrs…uh… Mrs. Carner…" She looked at the woman's name plate. "Mrs. Carner, how much? Will this do?"

"Um. You're still $470 short. I'm afraid she will have to be held here until the court hearing on Monday," said Mrs. Carner. "Besides she still has a warrant for her unpaid parking tickets."

"What? Look lady, have a heart. How can you hold my child here like some criminal!"

"With all due respect, ma'am, your child-"

"Her name's Gina Keagan to you!"

Mrs. Carner faked a smile. "Your daughter has sold and used both alcohol and drugs. She also had the warrant from September, not to mention that she smells of marijuana, and she has three unpaid parking tickets. I'm afraid-"

"You're afraid what, Mrs. Carner?" Mrs. Keagan retorted.

"I'm afraid she has no way of getting out of this." Mrs. Carner said.

Mrs. Keagan looked like she was about to pounce on Mrs. Carner.

"At least not without the other $470," Mrs. Carner finished.

"Um, Ms. Keagan," I said, stepping out of what seemed to be a hiding place.

"I have $420 of the $470 that you want."

"You can take it…if you want." I remembered that none of the Keagans ever liked to be reminded that they needed money. It made them feel they were poorer than they already were.

"You don't have to pay me back," I continued. "Seeing Gina grow as a person will be my reward." Gina looked up from her hands that were covering her face.

"I should've never treated you wrong. You've always been a real friend of mine, even when I thought Keith and Pat were my real friends. You were always there for me. Thanks, Mia …and I'm sorry. I know we will never ever be so close again, but I will never forget this." Gina said through sobs. I could tell that she was truly grateful.

"You're saving my child!" Mrs. Keagan said, "You've always been a true friend." Her anger melted.

Mrs. Keagan rushed over to hug me. I could feel her tears of joy trickling down my shoulder. "You, Alexis Mia Miller are a true friend of God."

Dear Diary,

Today I helped get my old buddy, Gina, out of trouble. Even though she's free, she still has to perform a year of community service. We are best friends again, and it feels good to be together. Gina is going make it after all. She is getting tutored and going to counseling. When she puts her mind to it, she can be unstoppable. I learned what true friendship is. To help with her drug problem she goes to counselor at my church. My God can make a way out of no way. Little does Gina know it, but it wasn't me that helped her, but the Christ in me! Gina's life is finally going to turn around, and another lost soul is now saved!

—

I Am Amiable: Say unto wisdom, Thou art my sister; and call understanding thy kinswoman.

- PROVERBS 7:4

I Am Love

"Hold it right there, Kim, right there!"

I held my pose in front of the background wall of limes on set.

"Click! Click!" the camera snapped.

"Boo-yah!" Mike shouted. "We got it. She's going to win that award!" He stepped on to set and gave me a high five.

"I told you she was our girl, Mike." Marlene shouted to him. She turned back to me. "Here's a basket of limes, courtesy of 7Up."

"Thanks!" I told her. "Do you know where my mother-"

"Yes!" I heard my mother scream. "Didn't I tell you my Kimberly was amazing?" Mike was trying to leave but my mother was blocking him. "We did it! I knew my sweetie would be the best for the job. I mean it's only automatic! I mean we've been practicing for weeks now, so she could do the job like in her sleep." She reached the snack table where I was standing.

"Darling! We did it! I knew we could do it!" She was always referring to me as *us*.

I suddenly remembered my sister Zoe's science fair. "Uh, Mom!" I looked at my watch. "Zoe's science fair ends in an hour. If we hurry, we can still make the judging." I started packing my bags to go.

"Oh, Honey Bunny, Sharon's mom can take her home!" Mom said easily, grinning. "I mean, what are soccer carpooling moms for?"

"Mom!" I stood to face her. "Sharon's mom can't raise Zoe for you. At one point in your life, you have to be a mother."
"I grabbed my basket of limes and walked past Mike who was staring at my mom. I got into the car and flopped down on the seat.

Welcome to the life of Kim Stanly. I have an eleven year old sister, who is five years younger than me, named Megan, a sister, Zoe, and a brother, Luke, who are nine year-old twins. My dad died two years ago, and now I am my mom's only available support system. Lucky me. I model almost all the time to bring money into the household while she relives her childhood through me.

Mom is completely clueless when it comes to my brother and sisters, but somehow all up in my grill 24/7. Recently, she has been prouder than ever, since I launched my new career as the new model for All Natural 7Up. Double the opportunity means double the clinging, which means triple the hatred from Zoe, Megan and Luke. I don't get it! Every time they can't buy time with my mom, they act as if I'm the one who's ditching them. I mean, hello! I'm the bread person, or is it bread winner? I don't know, but I really need to stop thinking about it that way. She's making me think about myself too much with her annoying pep talks about how I'm her favorite.

"You know, this has to stop now," Mom said getting into the car.

"Who and why?" I asked sarcastically.

"You and your attitude."

"I wouldn't have an attitude if you would stop using me like crutches!"

"What?"

"I'm just saying that sometime in your life, you'll have to wake up and smell the roses. Someday, Megs, Zo, and Luke'll be married and you wouldn't even have remembered their middle names!"

"Kimmy! Let's not do this now, honey." She shifted in her seat. "Let's go and get some lunch. Yeah, a lunch'll make it *all* better!"

I rolled my eyes. Nothing would ever make her better.

* * *

"Thanks, Mrs. Martin!" Zoe, Megan, and Luke yelled while getting out of the car.

"Mom, we're home!" Megan yelled up the stairs.

"All right!" Mom yelled from her bedroom. "Don't disturb your sister; she's picking out her outfit for the Models United Awards Ceremony!" I could feel their eye rolls from in my room.

"Hey, Guys!" I said coming down the stairs. "Zoe, how was the science fair?"

"Good! How was the shoot?" Zoe asked, putting her project on the dining room table.

"Don't ask the enemy!" I heard Luke whisper.

"Oh, sorry!" Zoe responded.

"Guys, dinner's ready!" Mom shouted.

"What are we having?" Megan asked.

"Shrimp stir fry. Kim's favorite."

"What about my favorite, Mom?" Luke asked sadly.

"No mac and cheese!" Mom scolded.

Megan put the glasses on the kitchen table. "Why not?" she asked.

"Because it gives your sister gas and it's full of carbs!"

"I don't have gas, Mom!" Zoe said.

"No, not you. The breadwinner! Kimmy here has the awards ceremony. A.K.A the biggest moment in our lives…tomorrow, and she just can't have gas."

Megan, Zoe and Luke just stared at me, and I sat silently staring at the chipped paint on the ceiling.

"Let's eat! "

"Mom, you never asked me about my science fair!" Zoe said.

"Oh, yeah, that! I forgot."

"I proved that magma could float using popsicle sticks and a mirror, and you know what……I---"

"Oh, heavens!" Mom interrupted. "I forgot to book your sister's nail appointment. What time does Lydia close, Kimmy?" She got up from the table. "We can talk later, Zoe!"

She added to Zoe as she dashed out of the room.

"I hate you, Kim!" Megan shouted getting up from the table and spilling her grape juice all over the white cloth.

"Clean it up," I commanded. I couldn't stand there attitudes when they started acting like Mom's behavior was my fault..

"Don't worry, the juice won't stain your precious fingers," Zoe added.

"Ahhhhh!" I screamed. *Why me?*

＊ ＊ ＊

"Come on, Kim!" Mom yelled. "The show starts in three hours!"

"I'm coming!" I yelled down the stairs, clasping the bottom of my red, long halter silk dress.

"Are you ready?" I asked Megan.

"Sure." She started putting on her dress shoes.

I was happy she was talking to me, because neither Zoe nor Luke had spoken to me since dinner last night.

"Get in the car!" Mom shouted. "And don't sit on Kim's dress!"

"Really, Mom?" Megan rolled her eyes.

We piled into the car, and after the short drive to California, we arrived at the Hampton Hall. I was so excited. I saw so many famous models and I suddenly felt famous just because they were there! There was Heidi Klum, Kate Moss, Tyra Banks and Twiggy!

We went inside and found our seats.

The lights dimmed on the stage and a chair slowly descended onto the stage carrying Beverly Johnson wearing a Vera Wang pleated blue dress.

"Good evening, and welcome to our Models United Awards Ceremony, which honors outstanding models for their achievements this year. The first category is the world's biggest smile. The Nominees are Sarah Bulfel for Colgate." Sarah's Colgate ad appeared on the TV monitors around the auditorium. "Amoni Turgate for Crest." Amoni's picture flashed onto the screens. "And...Daphne Greed for Arm and Hammer's Advanced White!" Daphne's ad was shown. "And the winner is... Sarah Bulfel!"

As Sarah's ad reappeared on the screens, she made her way through the crowd, while *Don't Stop the Music* by Rihanna played through the speakers. Beverly handed her a gold crown trophy.

Twiggy hugged her and handed her a certificate. In a daze, Sarah dizzily walked offstage.

"The next category is best pose. The nominees are Carry Lee for Juicy Couture perfume, Heaven on Earth." Carry, in a back bend pose with Juicy perfume bottles appeared on the screen. "Monica Rodriquez for Secret deodorant's Berry Blast..." Monica's picture of her diving backwards into a pool filled with Secret products appeared. "And Helen Springfield for Calvin Klein's new line of scarves!" Helen came onto the screen in a split with the heel of her back leg resting on top of her head wrapped in a Calvin Klein scarf. "And the winner is….Monica Rodriquez!" The crowd went wild as Monica's ad reappeared and she stepped on stage. She confidently strutted to the stage while *Best Song Ever* by One Direction played. Twiggy hugged her, handing her a certificate, while Beverly gave her the trophy. "The last category in the sixteen through nineteen year-old competition is the most theatrical shot. The nominees are Marie Curry for her Vera Wang ad." Marie's picture of her in a Vera Wang bathing suit swimming inside a perfume bottle appeared. "Kimberly Stanly for the 7Up ad." I popped up on the screen awkwardly balancing a tray on each arm. One was full of 7Up regular cans, which was the side that weighed me down. On the higher side was a tray full of 7Up Natural cans. My face was twisted and my eyes were wide. My body was covered in lemons and limes. I looked amazing.

I could feel the tension, or was it just my mom clinging on to my arm and biting her nails?

"And Michaela McHenderson for the Baby Phat line!" Michaela popped up half dressed like a baby, and half dressed in Baby Phat jeans with her gold heel hitting her head while she held a scorpion position. "And the winner is Kimberly Stan---!"

"Ahhhhhh!" My mom screamed, picking me up in a tight hug.. Of course, Luke was eyeballing me, but oh, well! I walked towards the stage, concentrating on placing one foot in front of the other. I made my way to the stage feeling like a princess as *Crazy Kids* by Ke$ha played overhead. When I got to the center platform, Beverly Johnson hugged me. Twiggy walked up to the microphone and said, "Excuse me, I would also like to add that Kimberly is the first sixteen year-old to win in her division. In all of the seven years this has been going on, no sixteen year-old girl has ever won this award. So, Kim Stanly, I congratulate you." She kissed my cheek, and I almost fainted!

I was handed a platinum trophy instead as the audience went wild, and I felt like I was on cloud nine.

"Kim, what's next for you?"

"Well," I responded, "I just signed a contract to model for Teen Vogue."

"And I believe you have the potential to do so!" Beverly said.

And that's just what I did. However, I forgot Jesus.......

* * *

"Ring! Ring!" my phone chirped. "Yes!" I answered.

"This is Marlene!"

"Speak!" I commanded. "A little to the left!" I commanded to my masseuse who was giving me a massage.

"What?"

"I meant the masseuse, duh. Talk faster!"

"Kim, how's it going. I know how happy you've been-"

"Happy? I'm now America's angel! Everyone wants me."

"I understand that! But I was wondering if---"

"Hold on," I said. "Zoe!" I screamed. "I need my iced tea."

One minute later Zoe showed up with my drink.

"Man, you are slow!"

"Shut up" said Zoe. "You think that since you are now popular, you can do whatever! That is your last command of the day." Zoe stomped off.

"Sooory, Mar!"

"Yeah, Kim, I think your sister is right. You have been acting differently ever since you won that award."

I hung up the phone.

Things were finally going well in my household. I know, yes, I became a brat, but I was now the official breadwinner. Without me, Megan couldn't afford her braces and Luke would still be sharing a room with Zoe! You couldn't blame me for acting this way, but my family did. Even my mom was frustrated with me for the first time. But since I thought that change was awesome, I didn't care what they thought.

* * *

It was the day I would become internationally famous. It was the day that my career counted on the most. It was my first Nike commercial, and man I was excited. I wanted to be a star so badly, and if everything worked right, I would be!

"Honey, let's go!" Mom shouted from downstairs.

"Way ahead of you!" I said excitedly, grabbing an apple from the fruit bowl and the keys to her car. I was not going to be late! "Mom, who else is coming?"

"Luke said he was out. Something about me being self-absorbed! Wacky isn't it?" Mom asked. She shook her head in disgust. "Anyway, Megan didn't want to go, and Zoe said she'll tag along, but only for the snack table offset. These kids are so blind! They can't see your value!" she said.

"Idiots!" I added.

"Let's go, Honey." She smiled at me. "ZOE!" she shouted. "GET DOWN HERE, NOW!"

Zoe came downstairs with my Marc Jacobs bag that weighed a ton. "Can I please drop it now?" she asked.

"No way," I said. "You're my assistant!" I dismissed her with the flick of my wrist.

"You know I didn't come for you, right?"

"Whatever!"

Zoe sat in the car, constantly interrupting Mom when she was trying to compliment me, and that bothered me, a lot. Could she be any more annoying? No. She couldn't appreciate me just once. Without me, she'd be wearing nothing but her underwear. I would just like to see at least one person appreciate me. In my mind I had a right to feel this way.

* * *

"Sometimes I like to let my shoes do the talking!" I smiled to the camera. "After all, you're only as good as your shoes, right?" I held up the new walking Nike shoe. "Nike….Just do it!" I winked coyly.

"That's a wrap!" Kelly, my director called. "Gorgeous! Now let's shoot this take outside and get some footage of you running! With the added effects, you'll be running on water, and it's sure to be a hit!" He gave me a high five.

I had done it. Everyone cheered me on, and everyone was happy. I nailed my second take, which was huge. I caused it. Me! Can you believe it?

We walked outside where cameras were waiting.

"Now, Kim run to that blue tape and then out of camera. The look on your face should be stunning and sneaky all at the same time. Can you do it?"

"Yeah, of course!"

"Now let's make some magic!" I noticed that the production manager and CEO of Nike, Joe, were sitting right next to Kelly, so the pressure was on.

I started on the side of the field and ran straight forward. My face was confident and I felt powerful! I ran some more and then out of view past the blue tape.

"It's a wrap!" Kelly said.

"Dude, that was pretty awesome." I said.

"Now last up, the photo that will billboard in all sporting stores in the nation!"

"Oh, yeah" I said. "Kelly, you mind if we take a five minute break? My throat's dry."

"Anything for my next big star!"

I walked over to the snack table and chugged down a cup of cold water. I was working my way back to set with a bag of Sun Chips when I heard the CEO, Joe, shout, "Wonderful! I love it!"

There Zoe was taking my billboard shot holding the new shoe. She was taking my picture. Mine. Kim Stanly, the superstar's shot!

"Joe. I understand, but I simply believe that Kim has the best portfolio!" Kelly argued under her breath.

"And now this girl," Joe pointed over at Zoe, "will have that same chance! It's beautiful."

"What in the flying fadoodle is going on??!" I asked.

"Joe!" Kelly prompted.

"I believe that little Zoe should take this photo. She'll bring in the cash." "Look at that face! She looks so innocent," he whined with a thick Italian accent.

"And so do I!" I fired back.

"Too bad. The decision is final. Maybe next year, Kim," Joe stated in a monotone, uninterested way.

I ran to Zoe. "You little monster! How could you destroy my opportunity? Why couldn't you just sit over there with your Barbies and play. What's wrong with you? Do you understand that because of you, my photo shoot is ruined? I'm the one bringing in the cash while you sit on your sorry butt!" Zoe was on her knees crying, but I didn't stop yelling. "You're a hideous excuse for a little girl who will never have a chance in this business, because you are a jealous, slimy little screw up!"

"Honey," Kelly said, kneeling in front of Zoe.

"Kim, stop it." Joe pulled me to the side, and all I saw was everyone comforting Zoe. I'm the one who needed comforting.

* * *

Hours later, the doorbell rang and I answered it. A bald man wearing a limo service tag stood before me. "I am here to pick up Ms. Megan, Ms. Zoe, and Mr. Luke." I looked past him and saw my Aunt Laura getting out of the limo. "Laura Sysco sent me." I gave him a confused look. He stared at me. "You know, the lady right there... with the long blond hair...."

"I know who she is!" I barked under my new designer sunglasses. "MOM!" I yelled.

Zoe, Luke and Megan walked downstairs with their suitcases and the driver carried them outside. My Mom was right behind them.

"Grace," my Aunt addressed my mother, looking long and thin as always. "I am here to pick up the kids. The arrangements have been made. The children are spending the summer with me in Montana." Even though we live in Nevada, on the same coast, Montana felt like a million light-years away.

"What?" my mom exploded.

"It's all arranged by our mother. She thinks it's a wonderful idea considering that the children are being neglected."

"Neglected?" Mom asked.

"Grace. You know it's true. It's time for you to start realizing that children are a gift from God, not books you throw on a shelf." With this, she swept her scarf around her neck, and went back outside.

Zoe came back in the house and said to me, "I would say 'bye' to you, but you are not worth my time."

* * *

May 21st

Dear diary,

I'm writing to you because that's what you do in Bible class. You write. Anyway, things are pretty crazy in my household! The silence is eating the life out of me! Mom's depressed, and I can't get Zoe's comment out of my head. It's been two weeks since they left and I miss them dearly. I still believe that she is wrong, because I am a compassionate human being with a heart as big as a lion. Kelly's words…, but I know something has to give. I am writing to you because I am supposed to write things in this Bible class that I am forced to go to. (Grandma has no life!) Mom goes, too, but only on weekdays. This is supposed to be cleansing, but my mind isn't cleansed! Who knows what I will do next? One thing is for sure though, I miss my family.

June 10th

Dear Diary,

Megan called mom today and they are doing fine. I think I am somehow starting to be renewed, as well. For one thing, I haven't talked about myself for two weeks now, so that is good. Also, mom is starting to realize that she was smothering me. She admits that she was wrong for not paying any attention to my sisters and brother. Bible school is actually working! Mrs. Oberg is teaching me how God doesn't want us to be self-centered. He wants us to be firm, but loving. She says that the same love Jesus had for the world is the same way we ought to treat our own family. I'm starting to understand it all, but I do not understand my problem.

June 15th

Dear Diary,

Mrs. Oberg is helping me uncover my problem. Like others in the group, I am more focused on myself and less focused on what's really important. I'm starting to learn the difference between wanting and needing. For example, I want my amazing career and to be the center of attention, but I need my family and a strong household. For the longest time, I have gotten these two mixed up, but I'm understanding it now. Mom is silently grieving, but she talked to me today. She explained that she was learning a similar lesson in her group, as well. She said all she wanted was for me to be happy, but the focus was on the wrong thing. She learned that she needed to pay attention to Megan, Zoe, and Luke, because

105

*if she did not, she'd miss out on their whole lives! We both are
starting to get the memo.*

June 20th

Dear Diary,

*Next week is the conclusion of group and we each get to
graduate! In order to complete the program, we needed to type a
one page report on our problem, what we did to fix it and what we
learned in group. My paper was about how I let my confidence take
over my body. Having confidence is one thing, but being cocky was
another. I wrote about how I hope to see my siblings again to make
everything right. I pray that I can keep on reading the Bible and
going to church because I realized even the most famous people
need Jesus! I long to see my family together, but this time, we will
know what the word family really means!* ☺

* * *

That weekend, Mom and I traveled to Aunt Laura's to see our
family.

"Hi, Ms. Grace! How are you today?" Myrtle, the maid piped
up.

"Fine. Thank you," Mom answered.

"The children are here, as is Ms. Laura. Come in!" We stepped
inside of the grand foyer and walked to the kitchen.

"This chicken is lovely Gertrude," Aunt Laura said in
admiration. She had on a little red dress and high white kitten
heels.

"Yeah, Gertrude!" Zoe agreed, sipping apple juice out of a
fancy glass. "I think it's your best."

"You say that every day!" Luke said, taking a bite of his noodles.

"Ms. Laura, Ms. Grace is here to see you," Myrtle said.

"Thank you, Myrtle," Aunt Laurel said. Myrtle left the room. "Hello, Grace. I believe you wish to see the children."

"Yes, please. I wanted to know if the children are ready to come home. We are ready, right, Kim?"

"Right." I smiled.

"That's a bunch of bologna!" Zoe said. She dropped her cloth napkin on the table and fled up the glass staircase.

"Honey!" Aunt Laura jumped up.

"I got it," I said, walking up the stairs. Once there, I saw five bedrooms. I found the one that said Zoe's name on the door in glitter and entered. It was amazing! There was tan furniture everywhere and there were pictures of the four of them on her wall. She walked up the stairs of the castle in the center of the room and on to the white Princess bed.

"I hate you!" she shouted.

"Zoe. I'm so sorry. I've been taking classes and everything!"

"What did they teach you?" she asked through tears. "How to pose for a camera? How to steal Mom's attention?"

I sighed. "Zoe. Before dad died, he told me one thing. You were too young to remember, but he said 'I want you four to stick together.' At the time, I had no idea what that meant, but I now know he meant that we have to support each other. I know you feel as if I'm a traitor, but I want you to know that I never meant to hurt you at all. Mom, mom was just messed up for a while. She loves you all so much!"

"Really?" Zoe hugged her teddy bear.

"Really. She thinks you are one terrific kid, and so do I!"

"You didn't think that when you screamed at me!"

"I was blind, Zoe. I had a lot of hatred and selfishness in my heart. I never meant what I said. I want to be there for you. I want to see you grow up and be a scientist just like dad!"

"You really think I can?"

"Either that, or you'd make one heck of an actress!" I tickled Zoe's stomach.

"God showed me that if I continued to treat you all like that, I would miss out on watching you grow up. I will always be here for you. Just know that you can count on me. Please forgive me, Zoe."

"I already did. I love you, Kimmy!"

"I love you, Zoe." I embraced her for a long time. I didn't know how much I missed her until I felt her arms wrapped around me.

"So can you come to my karate recital?"

"Not only will I do that," I pointed my finger in the air, "I'll make sure that *Mom* and I are in the first row!"

"Ya mean it?"

"Yes. I do."

And that's exactly what happened.

Dear Diary,

Today was Megan's ballet recital, and I sat in the very first center row! She looked so elegant, and I really enjoyed watching her. I never realized how much potential she had. Mom was cheering like a maniac and I saw Megan's face get red on stage, but then she smiled. I definitely learned how to show love. God showed love to the world, so the least I could do was respect and cherish my own family! I learned that without it no person can be happy. Family is more important than worldly things, although you might think otherwise. Most of all, I learned that if you really make an effort to make a happy home, you'll find that you will feel very good about yourself. I have to go! Luke needs help with his homework!

I Am Love: And above all things have fervent charity among yourselves: for charity shall cover the multitude of sins.

- I PETER 4:8

I Am Scared

It's three in the morning, and as hard as I try, I can't sleep. I cuddle up with my golden retriever, and I cry. Every day, I wish that I had never been born. In my house, there is no laughter, love, or peace. As silly as it might sound, I'm the reason it's that way.

Three hours later, it was time to wake up. On a normal day, like three months ago, my alarm clock would wake me up to a beautiful morning, full of challenges and sunshine. But that's not the story these days! What's the point of using an alarm clock when you have your own personal alarm at home? Your mom yelling at your dad, or vise versa, is loud enough! My parents wonder why I'm the way that I am. I'm so quiet, so self-conscious, and yet so alone. Well, if they would stop fighting, maybe they could figure it out.

After getting dressed, with my red, teary eyes I headed downstairs. As usual, Paige, my seventeen year-old sister, was propped up against the wall because she thought that the counter was germy and, as usual, my parents were sitting across from each other, threatening each other with their eyes. It was sickening.

"Beep!" That was Paige's ride waiting outside. She flew through the door to her emo boyfriend without a goodbye.

"Well, look at the time!" my mom said quickly. "I have to go to work. Bye, Karenna!" She kissed my forehead. "Don't forget your lunch in the fridge!" She looked at my father. "Harold," she said, annoyed.

My dad rolled his eyes. "Honey," he said to me, "I have to go now." He kissed my forehead. Following our normal routine, I rolled my eyes when he wasn't looking. Didn't anyone ever get tired of the same uncomfortable conversation every morning? I followed my mom into her office to help her load her books into the car. When she saw I was coming, she quickly moved a stack of papers off of her desk. What was going on?

* * *

"Karenna Smith, wake up this instant!" Someone shook me.

"What did I miss?" I asked with a yawn while the class erupted with laughter.

"Spaz!" A bunch of girls cried out. My teacher stormed over to the classroom phone. All I heard were the words, "Smith," "fell asleep," and "another time."

"Ms. Smith to the principal's office, now!" Mr. Ziegler shouted. I sulked out of the room hearing the kids still laughing.

When I got to the principal's office, I was greeted with the usual damp carpet smell and Mrs. Vernwood.

"Karenna, please sit down." She ushered me to a green chair and pulled out my manila folder from her desk. "Ms. Smith, I have been informed of the fact that you've been sleeping in class, lately"

I shifted uncomfortably in my seat. "Yeah… about that… It's not that class is boring or anything, but lately I haven't been sleeping."

"And why do suppose this is happening?"

I decided to spill my guts. After all, maybe she could help me. "It has been happening ever since my dad got this new job a while ago. He's never home and it feels weird, you know, without him. And, now my mom is always mad, and they always fight. My older sister, Paige, says that she knows what's happening, but I am too young for her to tell me. I'm always left wondering what is going on. They constantly fight, so I never get any sleep."

Mrs. Vernwood sighed and handed me a card, as if she suddenly grew bored of my story. "I think I know what's going on," she said. "But, I'm not too sure." The card had the phone number to one of our guidance counselors, Mr. Runkin. "I want you to see him. Maybe he can help you all. He's very good with family counseling. You can call him Monday through Friday from 8 A.M. to 4 P.M. Feel free to set up an appointment. I hope he can help you," she said standing up. "Take care, and come in if you have any questions."

"Thanks," I replied lethargically, leaving her damp-smelling office.

* * *

When I got home, Paige was there. We exchanged hi's like we did every day. I grabbed a snack and then went to my room to do homework. There'd been a time Paige used to help me with it. She didn't care how long or how hard it was. She was always there for me. Once, in the fifth grade, she blew off a whole essay to help me study for my spelling midterm. Now, her crazy boyfriends occupy her time, so there's none left for me.

Over the years, I have gotten used to it though. It was just me and my dog, Reese. She kept me company and she is the only thing on which I could depend. Everyone could be out fighting, but she stayed the same. It didn't help, however, that my dad had never wanted me to have Reese. He screamed at my mom for getting me a dog.

"We have two children! We don't need some dog!" he had said.

A couple of times, after I had gotten her, he tried to take her back while I was in school. With my family torn apart, I needed something that would always be there. I had God, too, which meant that somehow life would be okay.

I pulled out the card that Mrs. Vernwood had given me and I stared at it. I did need counseling! My whole family needed counseling! But who was I kidding? My dad 'King of the stubborn' going to counseling? My control freak of a mother going too? My family would never accept counseling; their ego was too strong.

"Knock, knock, knock!" Mom said as she opened the door. "Paige is at her boyfriend's, and your father is stuck at another conference again." She paused and frowned almost about to cry. "So, Reena, it's just you and me."

"Well, it looks like you have a lot of work to do," I told her. "I saw that huge stack of papers on your desk, before school."

She quickly looked up at me. She looked very nervous, so I decided to change the subject.

"You really let Paige go to Brian's?" I asked.

"She's so stressed with everything around here. We all are." She sighed heavily. "I thought that it would be good for her to get out of the house. But, he's so 'on-the-dark-side.'" She argued with herself. I felt bad for her. "I tried to warn your sister, but she won't listen." I was prepared to tune my mother's voice out because normally she'd start nagging about Paige and responsibility. Lucky for me, she was too upset to waste time rambling. "But, I can't deal with that drama right now."

"Oh." If she had asked me to repeat what she had just said, I'd be up the creek!

"Dinner is in fifteen minutes." She wiped a tear from her cheek and walked out of my room.

I could only imagine what was on those papers, probably anything from a divorce packet or just one of my mom's documents. Either way, I had to know.

* * *

Another sleepless night. Something told me that I needed to save my family from whatever those papers may have contained. I lay there for a moment listening to Paige's snores on the other side of my wall. I crawled out of my bed and tiptoed downstairs. I checked the coast to make sure I wouldn't get caught. It was pretty easy, since my mom slept like a baby. She was super tired from her day's work and once she fell asleep, she didn't wake-up until the morning. I walked to her office, but the papers were gone. I started going through her desk drawers.

"This is helpless!" I whispered. "I'm never going to find what I…" Then, I saw it! Under my mom's briefcase was a stack of divorce papers.

Suddenly, I felt lightheaded. I fell down to the ground holding my family's future in my hands. I knew it was coming, but I never expected it to be so soon. This was a disaster. I felt a wave of pain that was coming faster than Hurricane Katrina. I sat and cried for what seemed like hours. It was suddenly quiet in the room. Sure, I could hear my dad telling my mom to shut up because she was getting on him for coming in at 3:45 am, but all was still in the office.

"Fine!" I heard my father scream. He stormed down the stairs, grabbed his coat, and left. My mom ran after him in her robe and called after him. I could see him through our big picture window. He ignored her and swatted the air. Before long, I heard him drive away. Oh no! Mom was coming! I ran back to her desk, organized her papers, shoved the packet under the briefcase, and hid behind a couch in the corner of the room. She came in crying and swearing. She had never sworn because she said she loved God too much. I could only imagine how she felt. She swore again, called my dad a bastard, took off her wedding ring, then threw it towards the couch.

"Ouch!" I said quietly. The diamond hit my bare foot. I did not just talk! *Someone help me*! I thought. I think Mom was too mad to notice. She threw the papers on the ground and slammed the glass French doors behind her.

* * *

The next day was Saturday, a day that's as dull as dirty dishwasher. I woke up to hear my father leaving for 'work' as usual. The phone rang and my mom answered. I picked up an extension and found out that it was my mom's older sister, Sarah.

"Hello," my mom said quietly.

"Sandra, how are you?" she asked.

"I'm…..I'm fine, I guess."

"You don't sound fine!" Aunt Sarah said.

116

"I…."(Sniff! Sniff! Sniff!) "…am." My mom blew her nose.

"San! I'm coming over there right now. We're going to talk."

"Sarah, not today…please….just not now!"

"I'll take that as a 'Sure! I'm psyched!' I'm coming! See you in a few!" She hung up.

My mom thought that I was studying with my only friend, April, and that Paige was at the mall with her best friend Jackie. Paige was out, but not me. It was pretty easy to trick my mom who didn't pay me any mind.

Aunt Sarah came over at 2:00 sharp in her new Bentley that was as shiny as her Cover Girl lip gloss. She was wearing a little black dress and red heels, with a matching purse. She's the type of person who you think would say, "Oh, Dahhhrling," but she is really down to earth, considering her husband is as rich as Will Smith. I love her for being always true. You can always go to her for advice.

When she came inside, Aunt Sarah greeted my mom with an awkward hug. My mom poured them coffee, and served her famous homemade danishes. They sat in the sunroom. I sat watching from the scene through the landing of the stairs

"How are you feeling?" Aunt Sarah asked.

"Good, I guess." Mom stared into her coffee.

"Men!" Aunt Sarah mumbled. "How did Harold act when you told him about what you are planning to do?"

"He was horrible! He ran screaming!" Aunt Sarah frowned. "Am I a fool?" Mom asked.

"Sandra, you're doing what's best for you, Paige, and Karenna."

"Then how come I don't feel that way?" Mom challenged. She paused, "You don't know how it feels sharing your husband, wondering who she is, where he is, and why you ever got married!" Mom said. "Where did I go wrong? The first in the family to be divorced! I'm a failure! I'm a failure!"

"It will all be better in the morning," said Aunt Sarah. She hugged mom. Mom pulled away quickly.

"How?" asked mom while crying. "You don't get any special prizes for divorcing the father of your children."

"I'm sorry I brought it up."

"I have to be alone, Sarah. I have to be alone."

"Well, okay. I will call you later," my aunt said. She got up and left. My mom was through her ninth Kleenex by then. I wanted to come out of hiding and hug her, but I couldn't. Only God could help her now.

* * *

That night I went into my mother's room. She was alone and dad was still at 'work' so I thought it'd be a good time to tell her about Mr. Runkin.

"Mom," I said carefully. "I'm not as clueless as you think I am. I know what is going on."

"You do?" Mom asked.

"I think the neighbors would know by now!" I said sarcastically.

"Karenna, I'm sorry about the frustration you must be feeling right now. But it will all get better. I know that divorce doesn't seem easy…. trust me. We will get through this."

"I know, Mom." I paused, thinking. Maybe counseling was not the best solution for her. Maybe it would hurt the family more than help it. It was a chance that I would have to take. "Mom, my principal gave me the phone number of a counselor."

"I think that counseling would make things worse between your father and me."

"You never know until you try!" I quoted my mom in her high pitched voice.

She touched my nose. "You might be right about this," she said. "Okay, I'm in."

"Thanks, Mom!" I exclaimed. "But how do we get Dad to go?"

"I'll talk to him," she said confidently.

"No, Mom! I see what you 'talking to him' can lead to." I placed my hand on top of hers gently. "I'll try to talk to him. If anything, he'll listen to me," I said.

"Yes, you are probably right. Just do it…in the morning. No wait, after school. I just noticed, he's not here for either of these things. Have I really been that blind?"

I didn't want to give her the real answer, so I just shook my head and said, "No!"

"That will all change once you get him to go see that counselor," she said. "Be careful, dear. He bites sometimes." I could only imagine how he would bite my head off when I asked him.

* * *

After a silent and awkward dinner in which my dad had texted my mother that he was going out 'buying supplies for our pool' after work, I decided to wait for him to come home.

"Uh, dad," I stuttered, "Can I talk to you?"

He took a second to stop searching for something in his office to glance at me. "I would say yes, but Donna is expecting me at her house in a few minutes." He looked very worried for a second. "Did I just say that?" he said in a whisper. "Anyway, can you hold these?" he asked, giving me a stack of documents from his filing cabinet. I took the papers.

Wait! Donna? It couldn't be beautiful brunette Donna from his firm?

His office phone rang.

"Hold on," he said. "I have to take this."

He rolled his office chair around to face the wall. I sat down on one of his other chairs and looked around. I found his secret filing cabinet that he thought I knew nothing about. He was involved in his conversation and left the room. I quickly looked through one of his drawers. After a desperate 40 seconds, I found what I was looking for. A picture of Donna and dad at a banquet, and Donna's three year-old son. Why did he have the same nose that I have? No. It's impossible. There is no way that Jacob could be Dad's kid!

All this time, I thought that dad had to babysit him every Thursday morning. He told us that he was helping her get back on her feet since her awful divorce a year ago. That explains it! Dad always left with Donna when she came to pick her son up from my house. This was too much for me.

I grabbed the quickest thing I could find, a glass frame of a family portrait on his desk, and flung it across the room. I fell to my knees.

Dad came rushing up behind me.

"I heard glass. What happened?"

"How could you? You're crazy! Don't talk to me right now." I screamed. "DON'T talk to me!" I ripped the picture of Dad and Donna and *their* son and threw it at his face.

"What do you mean 'don't talk to you'? I can do whatever I want. I am your father."

When he saw that I wouldn't be back down, he said something that I'll never forget. "At least I'm not the one with an incompetent mother, a useless sister, and a filthy dog!"

"I hate you!" I said, running out of the room. I grabbed my coat and ran outside. I ran past our driveway, through the rain and wind. I ran until I could run no more because of my asthma. I stopped and hunched over to breathe. I looked back at my driveway and saw Dad running after me.

"Don't worry." I shrieked. "I won't tell your precious secret." I started running again, even though the rain blocked my vision. I ran another block to my friend April's house and pounded on the door.

Her mom opened the door. "Oh, hi, Honey," she said. "April's not here. She had field hockey practice."

"Oh, thank-you," I sputtered. I could only go home because Mom said that since she didn't know much about my other friend's parents, I couldn't go to their houses alone.

I took the long way home. Right foot, left foot, I thought. Breathe, just breathe. So I did, and it didn't help. Why me?

* * *

When I turned on to my block, I saw the police at my house. Oh no! I broke into a run to get home as quickly as possible.

"Oh, dear God," Mom said. She ran over to me and squeezed me tightly.

"Well, ma'am, it looks like she's safe." said a heavy cop.

"Thank-you," Mom said.

My dad's eyes were flaming red. He couldn't stop glaring at me. "You could've gotten yourself killed!" he screamed. "What were you thinking?"

"I---"

"Oh, you shut up, Harold," Mom shouted. "If it weren't for you she would've been home!"

All of a sudden, they started to yell back and forth at each other. I had to keep on turning my head every time they each spoke. It was too much!

"Stop," I yelled. "Mom, get a hold of yourself!"

"You heard her," Dad interjected.

"And you, Dad, you, get out of here! We don't need you or your brunette and son!" I scurried up the staircase and into my room. Reese was there to greet me. I flopped on my bed and curled up with her.

* * *

When I heard a sound, I stiffened. Wow! It was already 2:36 in the morning, but Reese wasn't on my bed. I got up. "Reese," I called out. "Come here, girl!" Maybe, she went downstairs. I ran downstairs, and turned the lights on. There she was. She was sleeping. I ran over to her and rested my head on her stomach. She wasn't panting like she normally did when she slept.

"Mom!" I screamed, running upstairs. I burst through her door and bounced on her bed. "Mom, get up!" It took three tries to wake her up, but once she heard me, she sprang to life. We ran downstairs. We tried to wake Reese up millions of ways, but she would not move.

"Honey," Mom said, soothingly.

"I know, Mom, I know….. Just don't say it." She gave me a kiss on the forehead, and a big hug.

* * *

January ninth was the worst day of my life. It was Reese's funeral. How could something that you loved be gone in a flash? How does a situation so bad become worse?

Dad was surprisingly there standing six feet from my sad mother in our small yard. I couldn't say more than two sentences without crying, so I let Mom talk. She was crying so hard that you would've thought a human died. We sang a song and then Mom prayed. Dad watched us, not singing or praying. You'd think at a funeral everybody grieves and mourns. Well, not the Smith family. Mom was bawling and using her hands to express her feelings about Reese. Paige even seemed into it, considering Mom said "no" to her when she'd ask to go with her friends to get her bellybutton pierced two hours before. Scratch that, Paige just asked to be excused. But realistically, I knew that she was going inside to text Brian.

"Honey," said mom. "Do you have anything to add before we cover Reese?"

"No" I sputtered. "Do it without me! I can't watch." I ran into the house. When I got to my room, Paige was waiting for me.

"C'mere" she said, her arms out wide. I ran to her and she gave me a squeeze.

"Kid, I know how you feel."

"You do?"

She ruffled my hair. "Yes."

"Yeah, right!"

"Well when I was three, before you were born, I had a beagle named Sam. He was everything to me. I trained him, fed him and groomed him every evening."

"Where are you going with this?" I figured her only purpose was to make me sad.

"Wait and see," she said. "I was just getting to that. When I went to summer camp, Dad was supposed to feed Sam. Well, when I came back from camp, Dad said he was gone. But I knew better. I didn't tell anyone that I saw a box of Hershey chocolate bars in the garbage can in the back yard. Obviously Sam 'mysteriously' found his way to the chocolate on the top shelf in the pantry. I didn't tell Mom because when she got mad…" She paused and widened her eyes. "He got mad…and you know what I mean when I say MAD! Mom was so upset that she bought Reese 3 years later. Dad couldn't take it! Between you and me, he went out for a drink. He said that he wasn't ready to raise a family and the dog wasn't helping at all.

"You mean to tell me that Dad could've had something to do with Reese?" I asked.

"He was really mad that you found out about you know who, so he went out for a drink and came back before you came home!"

"No! Nonono! He wouldn't! He wouldn't! He wouldn't!" I kept repeating over and over again.

"I'm sorry. I should've never said a thing," Paige said, looking at the floor.

"No," I said. "Thank-you for saying something. There's only one way to find out the truth."

"The garbage," we both said at the same time.

* * *

That night, when everyone was asleep, Paige silently walked into my room.

"Let's go," she said. I was already dressed under my night shirt. I put my sneakers on. Paige threw me a flashlight. I barely caught it. "Don't drop it" she warned.

We crept downstairs, and Paige slowly opened the back door after turning off the alarm. We raced outside like bandits to where Reese's play area once was. Then, I ran to the trash can. I remembered that my dad was good at hiding things in the dumpster, like that time when Mom made her meatloaf.

That night she slaved in the kitchen only to find out that she set the oven timer for an hour, but that she hadn't heard it go off. She had taken it out after three hours, instead. Dad faked that he was eating, said it was her best and then later buried it in the backyard dumpster. He didn't know that I was watching.

Paige passed me some latex gloves. She lifted the lid and held her nose.

"Ewww!" we both whispered.

"Reena, hurry up," Paige said, still holding her breath. We took turns taking things out of the garbage. We found 3 bulk boxes of snacks like Teddy Grahams and Jello, my old baseball mitt, Daddy's beat up lawn chairs and lots of small trash.

"P," I said, "this is hopeless! We are never gonna find anything and it's..." I glanced at my watch, "after three in the morning.

"Hold on! I think I have it." Sure enough she held in her hand a half used container of Betty Crocker chocolate frosting. Dad must have fed all of the chocolate to Reese. He killed her. Without thinking, I tore it out of her hand. I stomped on it about ten times. "I hate you! I hate you!" I kept repeating. By the time I was done my temper tantrum, I was crying a river. And no...I wasn't imitating Justin Timberlake.

* * *

"Ms. Smith! Get up now!" Mrs. Cook shook me. "I have one word for you-DETENTION," she hissed. She handed me two detention slips that were to be signed.

"Fix your hair." She commanded. When I touched my hair, I was stunned. I knew that I was a rough sleeper, but good, Lord, my hair wasn't even in a scrunchie anymore. I looked like Mufasa from the Lion King. The class howled while I fixed my hair.

"Ms. Smith, I won't even begin to list your consequences! Detentions and six demerits! Hopefully, that'll suit your fancy!" She glared at me. "And if you don't straighten up, I have a wonderful place for you this summer. Do you care to join me for summer school?" Yes, I thought. It was either there or prison, A.K.A my house.

* * *

"Sandra," my dad said while getting up from the dinner table, "I'm not eating. Leave a plate, and I'll eat it later." He reached into my mom's handbag and took her keys.

"Get out of my bag!" Mom shouted. My dad turned around, puzzled. He was used to being what Brittney Spears called a 'Womanizer.' Mom had never stood up for herself, but she wouldn't continue playing the charade that everything was fine anymore.

"Look, shut up! I'm taking the keys!" he said.

"I said no, Harold!" Mom screamed. She snatched the keys out of his hands. He slapped her face! He snatched the keys! And then, he ran for the door.

"Kids, go to bed!" Mom shouted at Paige and me.

"But, Mom---" I whined.

"I said go to bed. Everything will be fine." As soon as we were out of sight, the fighting continued. But this time, Mom was winning verbally. Dad slammed doors. He sat in the car for a while. Then, he took off in our Chevy.

* * *

I crouched down in time to hear the car door close. Man, dad's car reeked and it smelled like beer! Hiding out in the trunk of his car was the worst decision ever. And guess where we were parked? Harry's Bar! *The* Harry's bar in which two men got drunk and ended up fighting; one guy died! As much as I want to knock some sense into my dad, I thought about going in and pulling him out. What would happen if I did try to get him to leave? Would he be so drunk that he would push me or curse me out? I didn't care.

I unlocked the car doors and stormed into Harry's bar. As soon as I entered, I heard Carrie Underwood's song *Before He Cheats* blasting through the speakers. I immediately spotted my dad. He was watching the sports channel and sipping beer with the bartender. "Shut up and listen to the song!" I wanted to scream. Mom is going to do what Carrie Underwood is saying, to your car!

I walked up to him and patted him on the shoulders. "Hhhhow did yooou get heeeere?" he asked with the smell of alcohol coming through his pores.

"It's not important," I said. "You need to get out of here," I said, trying to help him stand up.

"Get your friggin' hands off of me!" he growled. He had never said that to me before. I wasn't going to cry, but suddenly my sadness turned into rage.

"You know what, you coward? I came to help you! And while I'm at it, I know what you did to Reese. I hate you! I hate you! You are a liar and a cheater. I could kill you for what you did to Mom. You have no concern for anyone but yourself. You are scum!" I screamed. I didn't stay long enough to see his reaction. I left and slammed the doors.

I didn't care if Harry's bar was across from my home town! I ran anyway. This time, I wasn't going to stop running.

* * *

In the middle of the night, I heard the garage door open. At 4:49 am! Oh well, I'll let the old man deal with his own problems. If he comes here and Mom kicks his butt, so what?! If he wakes up in the morning with bruises because when he was going upstairs stoned and bumped his head several times on the wall, so what. Why care? Why try? He never gives us respect, so why should I?

I realize that I am shouting. Should I love him? Should I hate him? What do I do? I'm scared for him! One day, he'll get into an accident because he drank and drove! The bottom line is I was scared. I was so scared.

I heard a knock on my door, and in walked my dad.

"We need to talk," he said sternly.

"I don't talk to drunk men," I said.

"I'm fine now, believe me. Just look, we need to talk."

Against my better judgment, I crawled out of bed and followed him. I'll give him credit. He already had tea and muffins on the porch coffee table.

"Sit," he said.

I sat down, but my eyes never left him.

"Where do I start?" he said.

"Let's see,…should we talk about your brunette? Your divorce? Or maybe your dire need to drink and then poison my dog!"

He stood up. "Look Karenna, you listen here! I didn't want another dog! You three are more than enough!"

"And you look!" I said. "Mom had nothing to do with this. I wasn't ready to raise a family!" I mocked. "Sandra did this! Sandra did that! That's such crap! It was you. I heard you. How could you take away the one thing that made me happy? How could…"

"Okay, okay." he interrupted. "Sit down, Reena, and let me tell you a story." I sat down. Dad turned his chair towards mine. He sighed. "When I was just your age, my father would fight with my mother. When he got mad, he hit my mom and went out for a drink. He used to say that you are only a man if you can toast a drink to every problem of yours. I always said I wouldn't end up like my old man, but who was I kidding?" He paused "When I would get mad, I would say 'what would Dad do' when the whole time I should've asked 'what would Jesus do?'" He chuckled, "I would drink. I would drink and drink and drink! You know how you are taught in school that drinking is very bad? Well, I knew that drinking was bad, but I wanted to be like my father so I never stopped. I do stupid things when I drink. You know that, don't you?"

"Yeah, oh do I know!" I sighed.

"I'm guessing that my father's influence had a major affect on my life, but that doesn't top what I did to you."

"I really loved her, Dad." I started to cry.

He wiped a tear off of my check with his fingers. "I know, Honey. I realized what I did, but it was too late. I'm going to be getting help. I've been thinking about seeing that Mr. Runkin that your mom told me about."

"Dad," I sniffled. "I'm scared. I don't know whether you are happy or sad or angry!"

"Donna's gone."

"What?"

"Donna left. I thought I needed a friend, someone to talk to, but she just got to be too much. It didn't work out. I want you to know that nothing happened between us. Her son isn't mine, I swear. She had Jacob before she met me. I just needed a friend and she just needed guidance. I let it get out of hand. And... I'm sorry. I am truly sorry. I need help, Reena. I need help from God. I am a sinner, and I admit that I haven't been a man of God. Kareena, I will change because if I don't, who will take care of my family? I will change. I will. Will you help me? I'm so sorry. I'm so sorry."

"It's okay," I stuttered, "but I need to know. Do you forgive me?"

"What?" he asked.

"I wasn't the most supportive daughter, and I'm sorry, too."

"Karenna," he held out his arms wide and I fell into them.

"You know what I want to do?" he asked. "I want to reserve Sunday afternoons just for us!"

"Really?" I asked.

"Yeah. We could see a movie, go bowling, anything you like."

"I would like that," I said

"But first, I have to apologize to your mother. I have to make it up to her. I'm going to take her on a vacation, maybe Costa Rica. But when we come back, you and I have a date."

* * *

Six months later, my parents had graduated from their counseling program. Mr. Runkin had been able to work a miracle and got my parents communicating again. There were no more secrets. Everything just felt so much better now. Paige who had agreed to see Mr. Runkin once a week with me even broke up with Brian! I could definitely see a change in her too.

"Beep, beep!" My dad honked the car horn.

"Come on, Sandra!" Dad called.

"I'm coming!" Mom yelled back.

Paige and I were just finished loading suitcases into the car and saying our goodbyes. I can't believe it's been six months. A lot has changed since then. When dad got to me, he said, "Kiddo, when I get back, it's you and me." I had no idea what he had in mind, but I just smiled and took it all in.

Dear Diary,

Today was my first outing with Dad. We went skating from noon until three. It was so funny when we fell together! We cracked up and took pictures. Afterwards, we went to Friendly's for ice cream. I ordered my usual Mint Chocolate Chip ice cream with fudge and a cherry, and so did dad. We laughed all the way home while singing with the radio. After today, I realized that I was scared for my dad, but God turned him around into a better man. My fear kept me from taking a step to help my family. I was scared that a simple gesture of leadership would only push my parents further apart. I should have talked them into counseling a lot sooner. I think that the change in my father is making me a better person. Next week, we are going to see a new movie. Well, I have to go! The basketball game is coming on, and Dad saved me a seat!

I Am Scared: *Trust in the LORD with all thine heart; and lean not unto thine own understanding. In all thy ways acknowledge him, and he shall direct thy paths.*

- Proverbs 3:5-6

I Am Healthy

"Order up! One fat-free vanilla shake with whipped cream drizzled in low-fat caramel," shouted the cashier to the wild crowd at Bertucci's Ice-cream Shop.

"Gawd. Louis! It's about time! I've been waiting for like three minutes and twenty seconds! You treat me like I'm some random customer. I'd ought to tell Daddy!" said snobby Rosalie Bertucci. "These poor people…. so desperate for a job," she thought aloud. "Why did Daddy hire such deprived souls?" Rosalie said. She took out her nail file and examined her perfectly polished manicure just as she had done two minutes before.

"No! Please don't tell Mr. Bertucci, please!" Louis begged.

"Whatevs." Rosalie snatched her custom milkshake and looked in my direction, but through me. She was giving all of her attention to a college-aged waiter with her unbelievably beautiful, commercial smile.

"Rosa, Brenda said to meet at her house at 3:00 to discuss the summer bash plans. It's…" I looked at the ice-cream scoop shaped clock. "…3:16!"

"Gawd, Tina! Patience. Wait in the limo!" she snapped at me. I started to stomp off to the limo. She was such a diva.

"Oh, and tell George I'll come when I feel like it!"

This was Rosalie Bertucci's 17th command of the week. And it was only Tuesday! I wanted to just snatch all of her "perfect honey blond" highlights from her spoiled little head. Now while I played the role of the servant girl, she was flirting with a waiter! Of course, I wanted to kick her butt, extreme athlete style, but Rosalie told me that if I even thought of turning my back on her and give up playing the game 'Rosa's way' she would show everyone in school embarrassing photos of me drooling at her sleepover, and she would tell everyone that I was adopted when I was one. She would also plaster my seventh grade photo of me with bacon in my braces all over Facebook. I did not dare mess with her because it could ruin my reputation. I never wanted anyone to know that my parents had given me away because they were too young.

Ever since beautiful and talented Brenda Rodriquez moved to town last year, Rosalie treated me like trash and Brenda as royalty. At her private sleepovers in her hotel, Rosalie and Brenda would paint their nails with a new nail polish. I would be stuck using the sticky ugly nail polish from three years back! When we played games with Claire, Rosalie's nanny, and Isa, Rosa's sister, I was always chosen last. When we would all visit her spa, everyone got to choose their kind of mask. Rosalie chose for me. It was always the worst selection: green peas and squash. I even had to use the bathroom last!

I don't know what went wrong. I was always so kind to her. I guess everyone experiences that one girl who drives them crazy. But Rosalie Bertucci, well, she was like having ten snobs rolled into one. We were so close until seventh grade. Everything changed for the worst. The popularity started to get to her head. She started liking lobster in butter sauce or sushi, rather than things like hotdogs or PB&J. Rosalie went from tomboy to Miss America. She wanted to have tea parties with her mom, rather than going skating with me. Bottom line, she went from good person to a nasty witch in one year. This year Rosalie ruled our high school like a senior even though she was still a freshman. She was the Queen Elizabeth of my high school. Even a popular athlete like me couldn't top that!

I had always wanted to venture out and maybe meet new friends of my own, but behind Rosa's charm was an evil girl who could expose my secrets whenever she wanted to. And she would if I crossed her. She wanted me as her sidekick, and she wouldn't have it any other way. Pretty evil, huh?

I snapped out of reflection when Rosa slammed the car door and rolled her window down.

"Bye, Brad!" she said, waving her hand as if she were Miss America. She said it so sweetly that I thought I might puke all over her Louis Vuitton denim blazer.

"Oh, Tina….window!" She looked at her window and motioned me to roll it up. I rolled up the window as we drove off and rolled my eyes when she wasn't looking.

"So Tina, what should this party have besides …everything?" she asked openly. "Ice-sculptures from Rome, balloon rides across town, amusement park rides, famous guests, a D.J., frozen treats … all compliments of Daddy of course. This party will be off the hook! Right, T?"

"Uh huh," I said with a fake smile.

"What should the invites look like? I thought about satin beach balls with a little white umbrella, but Brenda already said that she had it covered! Oh my God! I can't wait for this party! Can't wait!" She clapped her hands with delight. "Right, Tina?"

"Sure." I looked through her.

Rosalie kept saying the same thing over and over again about how the party would be one to remember.

"Yeah, like your embarrassing pictures from way before you joined a gym and got skinny. I like that video of you tripping over your shoelace and spilling coffee on Ms. Tyler in fifth grade!" I longed to shout at her. I mean really, she had looked like a watermelon. Plus, no one knew that she used to sneak her mother's diet pills, because of her obsession with losing weight!

I was extremely happy when the car came to a stop in front of Brenda's million dollar mansion. Brenda ran outside wearing her latest getup: a silver romper and black and blue knee high socks.

"Hey, Rosalie!" Rosa and Brenda exchanged kisses as if they were French.

"Hi, Tina!" Brenda gave me a hug. "Well, let's not waste any time! The party is in two weeks," Brenda announced. She led us into her huge family room and sat down on her favorite chair.

Brenda worked the money magic. Rosa called and made reservations. I designed and printed the invitations. By the time it was 9:00, the invitations were sent out, the special magic was paid for, and arrangements for Rosa's description of "everything" were made.

After a dinner of shrimp linguini and tiramisu, George drove me home.

A red Chevy was parked outside of my house in the driveway. I wondered who that could possibly be; hopefully it wasn't my crazy grandma.

When I went into the house, I saw three odd people sitting in the family room. They looked like a hot mess! A girl about my age with poopy brown hair and ugly overalls sat on the couch looking at the floor. When she did look up, I saw that she wore glasses. She wore overalls the size of my dad's pants. If she lost the glasses and maybe actually combed her hair, she might look presentable.

"Tina, these are the Thompsons. They are my real estate clients," my mother said.

"Hi," I said in a cheery voice.

"How do you do?" a middle aged lady said.

"I've heard a lot about you all. You just bought the house two doors down, right?"

"Yes, you're right," the man said. "A good girl you have here."

"Hi, I'm Kara," the woman said. "This is my husband, Anthony, and this is our daughter, Brittney" The Brittney girl looked up and waved shyly.

"Well, Tina, dear, why don't you take Brittney to your room, so we can take care of some business?" mom asked.

"Sure. Come on, Brittney," I said, motioning her to follow me.

When we got to my room, Brittney looked as if she were going to faint. As if a wooden floored room with rugs from Egypt, curtains from Peru, an iHome, Mac laptop, a huge marble floored bathroom, a king-sized bed with a canopy, a huge flat screen TV, and a sunken waiting room were items only tangible on Mars!

"Your room is amazing!" she exclaimed.

"Thanks!" I said, not sure what the big deal was. "So, where did you move from?"

"I moved from New Jersey."

"New Jersey to California is a far distance."

"I lived on a huge farm."

"Wow."

"I miss my friends. And my pony, Brownie."

"You have a pony?" I screamed.

"Yeah, until she was bitten by something and had to be put down. I never wanted to come out of my house since then and this happened." She touched her stomach. "I'm sadly overweight. I wish that I could be normal again. Life's not easy when you're my size! I don't have many friends." She looked at the floor.

Too much information. I kinda felt bad. An idea quickly rushed to my brain, but I didn't give it any thought before I said it aloud. "I know! You can come to the End of the Year party that my friends and I are having. I can introduce you to my friends!"

Suddenly, I wanted to take it all back! What would everyone think of her? She'd be teased to death. But, I couldn't tell her to forget about it. She was gushing with joy. I would break all that was left of her spirit. Wow, would that be harsh. Man! I couldn't take it back.

"Thank you so much. My mom will be so excited." She ran over to me and gave me a hug.

"No problem!" I managed a fake smile. What did I just do?

* * *

The next day Rosalie, Brenda, Isa, and I were eating lunch when I decided to ask some questions.

"You know how you said that you want to start being nicer to the 'boring' kids in our school?" I asked Isa. "Well, this Brittney girl moved in two houses from mine. She's a little nervous about meeting new friends, so…"

"How does she look?" Rosalie asked, while staring at her reflection in her compact.

I ignored her and continued. "I invited her---"

"What does she look like, Tina?" she asked again.

"… to the party!" I tried to sound upbeat and happy.

"Ahem!" Brenda coughed. "How does she look? Are you like deaf or something?!" The only thing to do was lie.

"Well," I began, "she wears contacts, but sometimes, she wears glasses…"

"Glasses!" Isa squeaked in a high pitched voice.

"Yeah, I remember when you wore glasses! You looked like a friggin' dork-o-saurus!" Rosa told her sister. Isa rolled her eyes.

"She has nice brown hair, good teeth-"

"You're missing the basics. Is she thin like us or a Twinkie-lover like Felicia Burns?" Rosalie asked, pointing to Felicia with her fork. She was referring to the humongous bully that was always stealing from stores.

"She dresses nice. She has a nice house."

"Will you shut up already!" Brenda snapped. "Gawd! Is she thin like me?" She smiled like she was on a cosmetic commercial. "Or is she as big as suitcase? Tell us!"

I dug into my purse, played my *Call Me Maybe* ringtone and asked them all, "Is my phone ringing?" Ah! Saved by the 'ringing' phone. I pretend to talk on it.

"Hey, Janice!" I said. "What's that? Okay. Hold on!" I put my iPhone to my chest. "Guys, I have to take this. My Aunt Jane is very sick. I'll be right back."

"You have an Aunt Jane? Well, I do too! Why don't I, of all people, know about her?" Rosalie pretended to look disgusted.

"Um," I thought. "She married into the family …in the winter ….and moved to … Greece," I lied.

"Greece? I love Greece! I did a report on it and fell in love with that state!" Brenda said.

"Brenda, Greece is a country," Isa retorted.

"Same thing!" Brenda said, while flipping her black curly hair. "Anyhow, what part of Greece are you talking about?" I was happy to change the subject, but I didn't know the most basic facts about Greece!

"The southern region," I said

"Where in the region?" Maria asked.

"Don't know. Gotta Go. Janice is waiting. Bye bye!" I said, running out of the cafeteria. What would my friends think when they saw Brittney??

* * *

It was the last day of school and party day. I managed to stay away from Brittney for two weeks. She really thought she was my 'best friend.' My mom gave her my number and she called me a good 12 times since we first met. Stalker much? I would have to keep us separated as long as possible at the party.

All day long classes were about how to protect yourself during the summer, so I barely listened. The day flew by, but I had a feeling that the party wouldn't.

I was right. I arrived at the party with Brittney, who was wearing this awfully ugly black and red striped t-shirt, while I was wearing a pink cocktail dress with pink wedges. I told Brittney I had to 'freshen up!' I was really hanging out with the famous guests. Mr. Bertucci had the Black Eyed Peas perform. It was even better than seeing their tour, which Mr. Bertucci got us backstage passes to.

I suddenly felt a hand on my back.

"Tina, it's time to welcome everyone. Let's go!" Rosalie said. She grabbed my arm and pulled it to the back family room.

"Greetings from my family to yours. Have a great time! Feel free to request songs to the D.J. Enjoy! I'll turn it over to Brenda!" Rosalie smiled confidently.

"Thanks, Rosa. Hi everyone. I hope you enjoy yourselves. We put a lot of time into planning this! Well, like Rosalie said, enjoy!"

"Thank you!" Brenda said. Her extra white teeth blinded the crowd as she smiled.

I grabbed the microphone. "Hi! Thanks for coming. We love having you all here. Have a lot of fun! Remember to stop by the pool area and have some frozen treats compliments of Mr. Bertucci! Enjoy!"

I waved to the crowd and walked towards the punch bowl. All of a sudden I saw Brittney out of the corner of my eye. She was wearing oversized overalls that had stains all over them and dirty, brown Keds that used to be white. Oh Lord.

"Tina., I was looking all over for you. I want to go home, now, okay?" Brittney yelled in my face over the loud music.

Her eyes looked puffy from crying. I felt sorry for her.

"Okay. I'll get your purse out of the foyer closet. Be right back!" In a flash, I returned to Brittney.

"Let's go!" I said. Rosalie swooshed in front of the door.

"Well…well…well! What do we have here? Well, let's see? A girl that should be entertaining the guests and helping out in the kitchen, and … a slime-ball!?

"Let's go, Tina," she said tugging at my dress.

"Rosalie, I have to drop her off."

"Don't give me that crap. Stop with your stupid charity case. She should be buffing my floors with the rest of the maids. Drop her and let's go. Now, do as I say or I will lose it!" Rosa shouted.

"Come on, stop faking! We all know that you don't need her! She might need you, but you certainly don't need her. I mean with that weight, that pig should be on my grill topped with relish! Tina, why her?" She laughed, cracking herself up. "She's not even worth two cents!" She flipped her ponytail and grabbed my arm. "Fergie is waiting!"

"Come on," I whispered to Brittney.

"Gawd!" Rosa shrieked. She was obviously drunk. As a light weight, she could get drunk with only one beer or one cup of punch.

She walked to the family room and grabbed the microphone.

"Look crowd. Look what we have here! An ugly, fat, porky Beverly Hillbilly! Beautiful, isn't it? Don't you just love her annoying company? Shouldn't that cow be at a farm making milk?" Rosalie asked. The crowd cracked up.

I knew I should have shut my mouth, but I couldn't! "Rosalie Marywood Bertucci! You're the spaz in this case! I bet the boys wouldn't like you if they saw this!" I reached for a big portrait of her– purposely tucked away on the mantle. It was a picture of Rosalie in her sixth grade year, with her face as blown up as a balloon. She had been severely overweight from grades fourth through sixth. At any mention of her obese days, Rosalie would become lightheaded and dizzy. Rosalie fell backwards as if in slow motion and landed in the fountain in the center of the room. Her Marc Jacobs t-shirt dress was drenched. The crowd exploded with laughter!

"This is better than last year's party!" a senior, Tom, called out.

"Yeah, we saw the beast of Rosalie unleashed and this ridiculous freak just got burned!" Kristy Cyprus squealed.

"Shut up, Crusty Kristy!" I demanded. She had been known for that in eighth grade when she had serious acne. "You see what happened to her? Do you want to join her in the kiddie pool?' I asked.

"Geez, Tina! I didn't mean it," Kristy said.

"Let's go, Brittney."

 Rosalie's evil gaze followed me and I could still feel it through the closed doors as we walked away.

* * *

Brittney and I were supposed to go to her house, but I led her to mine instead. When we got to my room, her anger radiated from her body.

"I'm such an idiot. Everyone hates me! If this happened at my old school, it was certain to happen at this one. This can't happen again. Not again!" She paced around my waiting room's table. "I'm going home now. I want to stay with my grandma. I need to get away! I'll never be welcomed in this place. Never." Brittney walked to the door with her head hung low. "Bye, Tina. Thanks for being my only friend." Brittney walked out in a daze. And I let her.

* * *

That night, I had a dream that Brittney became beautiful. She'd lost a lot of weight, wore contacts, and had new clothes. When she went to school, everyone's eyes were on her. She strutted across the hall with a confidence not even Rosalie had.

That morning I ran to her house. Call me insane, but I had a plan. I let myself in the back door, ran upstairs to her room and pushed the door wide open.

"Let's go! Let's go! Good morning!" I opened her curtains and let in the blinding sunlight. "We're going walking!" I said in a singsong voice. "Come on! Come on! Let's go!" She opened her eyes slowly.

"What are you doing here?" she asked.

"It's your lucky day. Meet your new trainer."

"What?" She reached for her glasses from the side table and put them on. "What. Who?"

"Me!"

"You're my what?"

"New personal trainer"

"And we are doing what?"

"Working out."

"Huh?"

"We are gonna get you in shape!"

"Seriously?" She gave me a look of doubt. "Could I really do this?"

"There's the enthusiasm!" I exclaimed. "Let's go!" The look she gave me said that she thought she was still dreaming. Surely, I couldn't be serious. To snap her back to reality, I pulled her arm as she got out of bed. "Wake up."

* * *

When she was finally awake and dressed, we started walking around the neighborhood. We walked around town for an hour. It was a beautiful day out! On our way back, we passed Rosa's house. Brittney told me that she was wrong to go to the party. And I told her that the only girl that would be sorry was Rosalie.

Every day we met at 8:30am. We walked from 8:30–10:30 around the neighborhood. I was her meal planner. I gave her a list of good foods to eat so she could lose weight. Less fats and sugars would really clear out all of that body fat. She went from chocolate chip pancakes to an egg omelet `a `la `Tina.

As for working out, we did the Zumba exercise programs. One hour every day was devoted to an exercise program of her choice. We even did Tae Bo and Hip Hop Abs. This routine continued for a month. Instead of eating out with her family, she came to my house for dinner since my mom was known as the spokeswoman for healthy living. When Brittney's parents went out, she knew she would get bored and eat too much because she had nothing else to do, so she came to my house. We made turkey sandwiches, had fruit salad for dessert, then twenty minutes later took a long jog.

The next month, I made her run. I started using my stopwatch to challenge her. And guess what? She was losing weight. Her stomach started shrinking! As we kept track of her daily progress, she was gaining confidence. She was really doing it. She talked her parents into getting her contacts. With more confidence came better hygiene habits. She washed her hair more often, and it looked amazing. Brittney pulled back her bangs, and what do you know her eyes where light brown. Who knew that a couple of changes could completely transform a girl completely? She was absolutely amazed, and so was I!

In August, we raced each other in the park every Wednesday. Before long, she was beating me. It was remarkable to see. Britt lost 40 pounds by just doing workouts and exercises and eating right. She looked better than Jennifer Hudson from Weight Watchers. Brittney even took control and cleansed her face. It helped that she was eating healthier, because healthier foods were keeping her body balanced. She looked like a completely different girl. We couldn't wait for the first day of school!

Here it was, the first day of 11th grade. Brittney was wearing a size 9 while, floral v-neck dress with a black belt attached, her gladiator black wedge heels. Brittney was more than ready, and I bought her black and silver jewelry to show her how proud that I was of her. I put her hair into a long fishtail braid and I added a cute silver barrette. We met at her house and before school we walked to a deli with lots of healthy choices to get breakfast. Even the customers stared at Brittney, and I knew that this would be nothing compared to how people in my school would react.

* * *

"Hey!" Ryan, a boy in my English class, said. "What are you doing this Saturday night, Tina? And uh who's your friend?!" He smiled at us.

"Uh, my *friend* is Brittney Thompson," I said. He did a double take.

"That's her? That's the girl from last year?!" He looked stunned. "Okay. You are lookin' good. Congrats on making the A-List, little lady!"

"Ha! I wouldn't want to be on your little "A-List," if you were the last boy on earth!" Brittney sighed. "Pathetic, isn't he?"

Ryan looked hurt. "Well, you can't blame me for trying." He sidestepped around her, looked her up and down and then walked away.

Out of nowhere, the junior cheer squad captain, Sasha Kelly, ran up to us. "Brittney Thompson. Love the outfit! OMG. The cheerleading squad is dying to have you!"

Brittney looked stunned. "Wow me! You know I don't have a cheer bone in my body." She flipped her braid to her side.

"Well, that's okay!" she said, looking at me. "If Tina here can work a miracle, well, so can I!" Sasha smiled mischievously.

"Hey!" Brittney said. "I may not have been the most beautiful girl in the world last year, but I'll always have more heart than you!"

Brittney winked and walked away from Sasha. Sasha let out a short gasp and ran away. Brittney was really a star, but she didn't forget where she came from!

* * *

After second period, Rosalie and Brenda spotted me. Brenda ran up to the two of us and Rosalie stared.

"Well! Is this the famous Brittney Thompson? Hi, I'm Brenda!" Brenda pushed past Rosa. "How are you? You look amazing, by the by."

"Oh, Brenda…lunch?" Rosalie called.

"I'll be there! Geez." In the background, Rosalie sucked her tongue. "So what was I saying? Do you want to come to my house for dinner tonight? The boys will be there, and they ah-dore you!"

"But what about Wednesday dinner with Rosalie?" I asked .

"Puh-lease, Rosalie who?" she said. "She was so holding me back. She is such a brat. I only hung out with her because her dad knew my dad. It was only polite. Somebody needs to teach her a lesson, for once," Brenda said in her best drama-queen voice. "So how about it?"

"You're not joining Rosa for lunch, are you?" I asked her.

"I told you, Rosa-who?" Brenda said, impatiently. Brittney and I smiled.

"Uh, Brenda, leave the charity case behind, and come to lunch," Rosalie commanded.

"No, thanks," Brittney said.

"You are so pathetic- hanging out with these losers. Wow. I thought you were better than that, you pitiful cow!"

"Who are you calling a cow?" Brenda demanded. "I'm not the one who couldn't fit in the rollercoaster carts in Six Flags when we were younger. Remember that the next time you want to call me a cow."

"Ouch!" a girl called. Everyone started to laugh and whisper. Rosalie stomped her foot and ran into the bathroom.

"So, what are you guys doing this Saturday?" Brenda asked.

"I heard about Ryan's party!"

"Please. Any party of his will be stupid once Rosalie shows up," I said.

"So, you're saying that you and Rosalie are done now for like good?" Brittney asked.

"I told you… Rosa who?" said Brenda. She smiled.

"We'll be just fine without her," I said.

As it turns out…. we were.

Dear Diary,

Today, I had dinner at Brittney's house. Her parents were so amazing. They even proposed a toast to welcome the new school year. As I reflect on what happened this summer I realize that I was Brittney's angel. I taught her how to be healthy. Brittney was now 40 pounds lighter because of her dedication and commitment. God helped me teach one girl how to be healthy and because of this, she can live a better life. I am so proud of her, and mom says that she's proud of me. I am so happy for Brittney. She really is her own person now. Brittney now has the tools to take her life to the next step, and hey, now I have a new best friend!

I Am Healthy: Know ye not that ye are the temple of God, and that the Spirit of God dwelleth in you? If any man defile the temple of God, him shall God destroy; for the temple of God is holy, which temple ye are.

- I Corinthians 3: 16-17

A Daily Routine
To Lose Weight the HEALTHY Way

Every morning –

Eat a nutritious breakfast: whole grain cereals, breakfast bars, toast, muffin, oatmeal, eggs, wheat waffles etc.

**Don't skip breakfast, or you'll be missing out on key nutrients for the day!

Exercising-

You should do it for at least 60 minutes a day.

Run in a local park

Take a walk through your neighborhood –It is good exercise!

Take the time to view your neighborhood and the world around you.

Do a workout video

Do it with a friend. It's a great way to have fun. There are plenty to choose from!

Vary them from day to day For example, one day do Tae Bo, the next day play Xbox Kinect, the Wii or try Zumba!

Watch what you eat!

Learn how to understand the labels on packaged foods. Not everything that looks healthy on a label is good for you. Visit the website www.mypyramid.gov to plan the right diet for you.

Remember, everyone is different! Not every workout plan and diet that works for others will be beneficial to you! Work out your own way and have fun with it!

Don't quit, stay positive, stay active, and stay HEALTHY!

I Am Focused

"So, mom, I was thinking I want to be a Pediatrician just like Mariah," Daria said.

"Why?" I asked. "Is it just because they make a lot of money?"

"Well, besides that, I love to help children."

"Well it's a big commitment, I hope you are up for a challenge!" her mom said.

"I know it is going to be hard, but I am."

"You can totally come to the medical seminar at the University of Pittsburgh with me at the end of the school year!" I said informing her about the summer program for potential Pediatricians.

"Yea, I would love to. I've been meaning to get involved in something like that."

"That's my girl!" Daria's mom exclaimed. "She is gonna be the first doctor in our family."

"I know she will," I agreed. "She is one of the smartest people I know."

"Oh, speaking of smart- mom can I go to Tracy's party tonight?"

"No, Daria! You know I need you to stay focused on your studies. It's a school night anyway! Why would you even ask me?

I mean, seriously, you know how I feel about you young people partying."

"Mom, take a breath! I was joking. I just wanted to see your reaction. You know how focused I am on school. Have I ever given a reason to worry, just once?"

"No." She sighed.

"Exactly, Mom. I know how important school is, besides you tell me every day!"

"Hey, I don't lecture you that much!" her mother said, defensively.

"Mariah, does she?" Daria asked.

"Kinda!" I joked.

We all laughed as Daria's mom threw a grape at her. When we finally settled down, Daria went back into the family room to finish her homework.

* * *

"Ding-ding! Ding-ding!" the oven chirped.

I had just finished baking my famous lemon cake with vanilla frosting in Food and Nutrition Ed for the end of the semester's Bertzon Bakery contest. I was determined to win the 'Best Cake' prize. The whole class was waiting on Stacey Stephens, a perfectionist, to finish her cake so we could start the judging.

"I'm done!" Stacey exclaimed. "Don't expect to win against my chocolate volcano cake!"

"Thank you, God! She's done," Daria exclaimed.

"Now ladies, line up at your tables. When I say to, everyone will visit each station in a counter-clockwise rotation. You will rate each cake on this ballot on a scale from one to ten then circle your favorite. Remember girls, let's not be biased. Vote fairly. Okay. Chop chop!" Mrs. Andrews clapped twice.

We all took our ballot sheets and rotated to our first stations. I stopped at Kate's table. She made a standard vanilla cake with too much butter. Yuck! I almost choked, and I had to drink a glass of water. I gave it a 4. I tasted Melinda's strawberry cake. It wasn't that bad. I gave it a 6. Next, was Bella's carrot cake, which, not surprisingly, was made from natural products. She used soy milk and I wanted to gag. I gave her a 3, for effort. Then I tasted Nicole's German chocolate pound cake, and it was sensational! I gave her a 10. Amber's was next. As usual, her fudge layered cake was loaded with sugar. It was diabetes in a slice, so I gave it a 2. Next I went to Daria's station and tasted her sweet potato cake. It was not her best idea. Although she was my best friend, I gave her a 5. Lastly, I arrived at Stacey's station. She was right; her cake was amazing. Still warm from the oven, her volcano fudge cake was to die for. She had the advantage of being a chef's daughter. Her family's name was legendary. If I could've given her a 20, I would have. I circled her name and handed my ballot in.

After waiting for everyone to finish completing their ballots, we gathered around for the results.

"Girls, I don't mean to upset anyone, but this year, I cannot attend the end of the year's cook-off sleepover. My husband just got back from Iraq, and he is sick. I am very sorry, and I hope you understand," Mrs. Andrews said.

Everyone gasped.

"Okay, the winner is…"

"Right now, we don't care. You can't come?" Stacey said.

"Is that all you care about?" Amber shouted. "Some tradition?"

"Since the president of our club is Stacey, she will host this year's cook-off."

The girls started cheering. I was frowning. I didn't want to go to Stacey's house. She had a reputation for getting drunk and getting others drunk, too. Marcia DuBola never drank a day of her life, but after Stacey's party, she chugged beer like a 250 pound man! Casey Carter, who was once a teacher's pet, started smoking after one sleepover at Stacey's. I didn't want to be caught drinking or with drugs at 17. My life was worth more than that. Using drugs and alcohol would mess up my mind, making it hard to reach my goal to become a Pediatrician. The best way to avoid getting caught in that drama was to not attend the party. I was willing to end a tradition, to preserve my life!

The best way to break the news was to text Daria. Surely, she'd understand.

I picked up my iPhone and composed my message.

Dar, My dad is coming home from Africa tomorrow. I'm sorry, but my mom is taking us out to celebrate at Wynona's Steak House. I can't go to the party.

Before I would regret it, I pushed the send button. It was a good enough reason to miss the party, but it was so stupid! How many 17 year-olds missed parties for family? Dar was too smart, and she would know I was lying. I should have just gone with the story that my stupid brother Aaron had the chicken pox from scouting in the woods and I was exposed to it. Stupid. Stupid. Stupid! I slapped my forehead.

A message popped up on my phone.

What!!! U can't miss the party. U can't

Okay maybe she didn't understand. I grabbed my phone and started typing angrily.

Sorry! My mom'll b mad. I hav to.

Couldn't she just go with it, already?

Fine! I'll cover for you… for your dad! I still don't like you!:)

Thank goodness. I was off the hook. I responded:

Thanks

I was safe… for now!

* * *

The next day, I woke up late and watched *Shake It Up* on Disney Channel with Aaron. I was relieved not to have to go to the party, even though a tradition would be broken. Mom was working an early morning shift delivering babies, so I was responsible for Aaron.

There was a sudden knock on the door. I assumed it was Aaron's annoying friend, Billy.

"Aaron, did you invite Lance over? Mom said that you needed to do all of your chores first, then invite Billy."

"I didn't invite Billy, Mariah. Chill!" he exclaimed.

I looked through the translucent glass door and saw Daria, her parents, and her brother Mike. On the doorstep, Mike was holding a party bag, and Daria "Welcome Home" balloons.

"Oh no!" I muttered.

"What?" Aaron said, walking to the door.

"Um… I kinda told Daria that Dad was home just so that I could stay home from a party."

"Well, you can't be rude. Let them in." He pushed past me and opened the door. He just wanted to see Mike. Gosh, he is so annoying!

"Follow my lead," I said, quickly before I could see them.

"Hi!" they said in unison.

"Hi…guys!" I said. "I'd love to chat ab-bout my dad and all. And I'm sure you do too, but he just left!" I smiled weakly. "Right Aaron?"

Since all of the gazes shifted to Aaron. I mouthed to him "Help me." He picked up the hint.

"Yeah! He did… to buy shaving cream and … medicine!" He smiled.

Idiot!

"Yeah right! Where is he really?" Daria asked.

"That was the real story. He went to buy shaving cream and…," I frowned. "Medicine."

"Okay!" she said, in a high pitched voice. "Mom, Dad, Mike, I'll take it from here!" When she thought I wasn't looking, she gave them a thumbs up.

"What was that for?" I asked.

"I knew you were lying. You sweat when you lie!"

"No, I don't!" I wiped sweat from my neck.

"Just tell me!" she whined.

"Tell you what?" I asked.

"I ditched the party to see your dad who I know is still in Africa on his business trip!" Daria smiled.

She won. I had to confess.

"Okay!" I sighed. "I don't want to go to Stacey's party because she's an alcoholic!"

"But… she can be responsible. I've seen it. Just give her a chance.

"She drinks and smokes. She gets in trouble, and keeps on drinking anyway." I paused. "There, I said it!"

"But, you know her parents are religious. They made her swear on a stack of Bibles that she'd never drink again. If she did, she would be grounded for a whole year!"

She laughed at the thought. "Relax!"

"You know Stace though. She does anything she wants – without getting caught! I don't know about this," I said nervously.

"I promise, if we even get a whiff of alcohol, we'll leave!"

I rolled my eyes. "Fine!" I said. "….but I won't like it!" I tried.

"Relax. God!" she laughed. "Get dressed. I promised, didn't I?"

"Well, yeah…"

"Exactly. Fierce!" she shouted and snapped her fingers. It was our thing, our inside joke from seventh grade.

"Fierce!" I said, and snapped my fingers. She gave me a fist pound, and then she pointed to the stairs.

I started up the stairs thinking that Daria just might not keep her promise.

* * *

When we pulled up to Stacey's driveway we could hear loud salsa music blasting from inside.

"Call me if you need me, girls." Daria's mom called out. We walked to the door and rang the bell.

After a few seconds, Nicole opened the door.

"Hey, Mariah. Hi Dar. Come on in! Let me take your sleeping bags. Go through this hallway, make a right, then another right, and that's where the girls are!"

"Thanks!" Daria exclaimed and gave Nicole a hug. We followed the directions and found the girls dancing to salsa music and eating spinach rolls.

"We didn't start yet. We were waiting for you guys," Melinda explained.

"Let the cooking begin!" Stacey shouted. "Nicole and I are captains. I represent the Diamonds and Nicole, the Pearls. Line up against the wall so we can pick teams!" We rushed to the wall.

"I'll take Amber!" Nicole said. Her best friend rushed over to her.

"Mariah" Stacey said.

"Kate"

"Melinda" Stacy said.

"I'll take Bella"

"And I'll take Dar!" I was so relieved that Daria was on Stacy's team with me.

It was all set. The Diamonds included their captain, Stacey and teammates Daria, Melinda, and me. The Pearls included their captain, Nicole and teammates Amber, Kate, and Bella.

"Diamonds will be in the downstairs kitchen. Pearls, upstairs kitchen. When I say 'go', you will get an apron from my maid, Kerri." Stacey motioned to a little middle aged woman. "This is the challenge: create a dish with catfish and three sides; any type of rice or vegetables, whatever you want. You have one hour to complete the first course, and for dessert, another hour. For dessert go crazy! Whatever your little hearts desire! My brothers will supply you with all of your alcohol needs. Vodka, beer, wine, champagne, rum, you name it. You never know what you might need!" she said cheerfully.

"Stace, I don't mean to be mean but, you…um SWORE!" Melinda spat.

"On a stack of Bibles!" Amber added.

"Girls! Relax. Will is supplying them, and he is 20!" she said not missing a beat.

"But he isn't 21!" I shouted.

"And we aren't either!" Zoë added.

"Ladies, relax. If we get caught---"

"You mean when *you* get caught," Daria corrected her.

"Whatevs! Look we have to get started!" Stacey said.

"Let's!" Nicole said.

Will gave each girl a supply of alcohol. When he got to me, I said, "No thanks." He gave me white wine anyway. I decided that this wouldn't be bad. I just wouldn't drink it, that's all.

When we Diamonds arrived in the downstairs kitchen, the cooking began. Stacey and I worked on peeling potatoes to roast them, while Melinda boiled the rice, and Daria peeled the carrots. It was a lot of fun! We pretended to be famous Italian chefs with accents. We took turns watching the clock and dancing to fast music.

Will suddenly slid down the railing of the stairs. He looked horrible! His face was pale, and his eyes were bulging out of their sockets.

"Come on!" he shouted. "Do you want to be amateurs or do you want to be real Italian chefs? He added a whole bottle of rum to the rice.

"Go, Will!" Stacey shouted. Next, he started chugging shots of Tequila from the basement bar.

"Go! Go! Go! Go!" They started chanting, Daria included.

"Daria!" I yelled at her. "Let's go! Will's obviously drunk. Come on!"

"So what! You heard Will. Let's be real chefs," Daria said cooly. She grabbed a shot and drank it .

"Go, Babe go!" Will said.

"Let's go! This party is whack," I said, in attempt to get her to come to her senses.

"No. You are!" Melinda exclaimed. Two empty bottles of beer were next to her, and she was drinking her third. I tried to pull Daria towards the door, but she pulled back and called me a jerk. She was on her fourth shot. It was all happening too fast. I felt like I was going to vomit.

"That's soooo good!" Daria said. "Will, pour me another one!"

"Ohhhhhh Willllll!" Stacey screamed, obviously drunk. "Go get Mom's lighter!"

She sipped her fourth beer.

"Yeahhhh!" she shouted. The three girls started making a conga line around the coffee table. They were uncoordinated, shifting from side to side, close to falling down. Will came back and Stacey lit a cigarette. By this time, Daria was on her eighth shot, Melinda, her fifth beer, and Stacey, her seventh beer. I was stunned! I ran upstairs to get some air.

Upstairs wasn't any better. The girls were belly dancing to Shakira's song, *Hips Don't Lie,* with glasses of red wine in one hand and a cigarette in the other. The ashtray on the table was filled with cigarette butts. I needed some air. I went back downstairs to get Daria, and leave. Daria, Will, Melinda, and Stacey were smoking. They started smashing beer bottles.

"Oppppaaaaa!" Daria dropped a glass plate on the wooden floor.

Forget this. I was going home!

"What's t-the mather, Mirah?" Stacey asked, lighting another cigarette. She caught my arm. "If you were a real Bertzon Baker, you'd drink with us!" She took her beer and splashed it onto my shirt.

"You're sick!" I shouted at her.

"Ya want one?" she asked.

"No!" I screamed. "Let me go, now!"

I quickly walked to the downstairs bathroom and dialed my mom's phone number. I had no other way of getting home.

"Shots! Everybody!" I could hear them all singing *Shots* by LMFAO from inside the bathroom. The music was blasting from Stacy's iHome, but I could still hear their chants and laughter over it. After the six tries to reach my mom, I decided that I would walk home. Nothing could be worse than sitting around and watching them act crazy and irresponsible.

When I got out of the bathroom, I found Daria dancing on top of the barstool, chugging more shots. She lost her balance and fell off of the counter. Will barely caught her.

"Woooops!" she shouted. "Thanks, Will! I loooove you!" she turned to me almost falling on top of me. "Stop being a sissy wuss! You can't act like such a boring Nun forever !"

"Daria! How could you do this to me, and yourself?" I turned and started running up the stairs. Someone patted me on the back.

I turned around about to say "What?" when Stacey tried to pour her shot in my mouth while keeping her balance on the step below mine.

I pushed Stacey away. Unable to keep her balance, she fell backwards down the wooden spiral staircase. Stacey fell on top of Daria, who was facing the basement wall. Daria fell on the wooden floor face first. She had the wind knocked out of her.

I ran down the stairs to get to her. I spotted a huge cut bulging with blood on her forehead. Her blood was dripping on my pants. "Daria!" I cried out. "Please! Please, please! Wake up!" I wasn't a doctor, but I knew this would be bad. I ran upstairs and called 911. She was unconscious.

* * *

When the ambulance arrived, Daria was still unconscious. I followed the crew outside and, of course, Stacey's parents showed up at that moment.

"What's going on, Mariah?" Stacey's mom said frantically while getting out of the car.

"Mrs. Stephens, we were just cooking. Will supplied alcohol and the girls got drunk. Stacey accidentally pushed Daria down the stairs, face first, and now she is unconscious. Will was arrested for serving alcohol to minors and underage drinking. The police took the other girls home."

"Oh my goodness!" Mrs. Stephens gasped.

"I'm very sorry!" I said. I was barely able to get any words out as my throat and face burned from crying. I patted her back and walked to the ambulance truck. Daria was strapped to a gurney, and she had tubes hooked to her arms. Her eyes were swollen and blood was dripping from her nose and ears. I rode with her in the ambulance truck.

When we got to the hospital, Daria was still not breathing on her own. A nurse called Daria's mother who had to be picked up by an officer since she couldn't concentrate while driving.

I wasn't allowed to see her. As I sat in the waiting room, I thought about Daria's promise. It was an easy promise to make, but a hard one to fulfill. I never realized that someone with such a big future ahead of her could be sucked into peer pressure so quickly.

"Ms. Anderson, Daria would like to see you now," a nurse said.

"She's awake?" I asked happily.

"Yes!" the nurse exclaimed. "This way." She ushered me down a narrow hallway.

When I entered the room, Daria's mom left.

"M-mariah?" Daria whispered sleepily. She could barely speak. It was hard to understand her slurred speech. "Oh, man. I am so sorry I got you into this. I'm sorry I drank. I don't know why, but I wanted to have more fun. I felt that I had to loosen up….you know? I'm sorry I got you into this. I feel so stu-" She started wheezing and coughing. "Please forgive me, Mariah. Don't drink. Don't be like me. It hurts. I have this huge pain… in my head…. and in…my heart." She sighed and started to cough.

"Uh, I'm sorry. You have to leave now," said a petite nurse who came into the room. "Visitation hours are over. She will be okay."

"You'll be fine," I said, trying to convince her and myself. She nodded slightly, and then she winced as a result of the headache from the minor movement.

"Fierce," she mumbled, not snapping her fingers.

"Fierce," I said, and snapped my fingers. This time, I gave her a light fist bump. I left the room, and her eyes followed mine.

Obviously, her condition wasn't going to get better. We both knew it.

* * *

That night, I couldn't sleep. I thought of Daria, unconscious. I tossed and turned. Surely, God would save her. At last, I drifted off into a heavy sleep. I dreamt of Daria alive and well.

My dream was interrupted when my mom woke me up at 1: 16 in the morning. She brought me into the kitchen where tea in fine china was on the table. What was going on?

"Mom, what's this?" I yawned.

"It's… Daria, honey.

"……yeah….." I said nervously. "What?"

"Honey, she went to be with the Lord."

"Huh?" I said, shocked. I knew what had happened. My brain could not wrap around this information. I just didn't want to face it.

"She passed due to alcohol poisoning and head trauma from the fall… I'm so sorry."

"No!" I corrected her. I ran to the door, and put my flip flops on. "I'm going to see her." I opened the door, but I was caught by my mother. "She's still alive!" I cried out.

"Baby, I'm sorry."

"Nooooo!" I screamed! "Nonono!" I hit the floor. "Why, God? Why?" I screeched. "No, I'm going to go and see her!" I got up and opened the door, but my mom blocked me.

"Mariah, Honey! She's dead!" She pulled me tight, and my tears spilled onto her chest.

"The most important thing is that, you stayed focused and remembered right from wrong." She said after a long silence.

"You did not give in to the peer pressure. I know it was hard and you are hurting now. But that could've been you. I could have lost my child." She started sobbing silently, and we stood there for a moment. "You did not give your soul up to the devil. I'm so proud of you. I love you. You become that Pediatrician. Do it for Daria. She would have wanted you to live that way!

Dear Diary,

Today was Daria's funeral. It was the saddest day ever. How could God do this to me? We were born on the same day, and we were best friends since the seventh grade. Why was this her fate? I will never know.

The most important lesson I learned was to stay focused. I could have given in and drank with the in-crowd. Instead, I didn't. Daria is a tragic example of what giving into peer pressure can do. I don't know why God let her go, but I know he had a reason. I decided to join the cause to fight teenage peer pressure. I will attend a club called Focusing Straight Ahead, which teaches teens how to just say no. It's a fun club and I tell Daria all about it every day.

I dedicate this diary to Daria Jessica Avery. May her tragedy save others who fall victim to peer pressure, every day.

I Am Focused: There hath no temptation taken you but such as is common to man: but God is faithful, who will not suffer you to be tempted above that ye are able; but will with the temptation also make a way to escape, that ye may be able to bear it.

- I CORINTHIANS 10:13

I Am Human

"Hi, honey!" Grandma Benny greeted me at the front door. She led me inside her house. "Sit!" she commanded. "Let me see that chemistry test of yours."

"Grandma," I whined. "Please not now."

"Why the whine, my girl? You are a seventeen year-old girl, not a baby." She furrowed her eyebrows. "Did you do well?"

"Well…" I took the test from my green tote bag. "Not really." I gave her the test.

"A 70?" she asked. "My goodness! Your father is going to have a cow."

"He won't even see it! He wouldn't care to. He's probably still with that little rich girl in France." I sighed.

"Amber, you know that your father's in France *on business*. At least that's what he told me."

"Grandma, he also told you that he was coming back today!"

"What is that supposed to mean?"

"He called me last night. He will be in France for another week." I frowned, leaning over the counter.

"Oh! Well you're welcome to stay here as long as you want. It's only me and your grandpa. Besides, it must be quite lonely with an empty house."

"Yeah, I guess."

"You don't mind staying the night on Friday and driving us to aerobics on Saturday morning, do you? You know how your grandpa injured his driving foot."

"Of course not, as long as I don't have to sleep in the witch's room, I'm ok!"

"Don't talk about your mama like she's some other folk."

"Sorry," I mumbled. "But, I'm glad she's in jail."

"Amber, I'd be glad also… if she wasn't my only daughter. You must stop talking about her."

"But---"

"But, nothing. Go and get the mail."

Annoyed, I walked outside to the old little white mail box. I found nothing but a small envelope. It was from the rehab center. It could only be from my mother. If it was another letter asking for us to bail her out of jail again, I was going to tear it into shreds! She caused me so much grief. I still think of her abusive attacks so much that sometimes I can't even sleep at night. One time she kicked me in the stomach, hit me in the face, and punched me in the chest when I was nine for coming home one minute later than 7:30 from a play date.

It all ended when she went for a jog and left me alone in the house. I called the cops and she was taken away. I was sent to live with my father in his home. I still remembered the day when I moved. The same night he had to fly to Europe for a meeting. Since then, I sucked it up and had to live by myself most of the time.

Because my father knew that he couldn't take care of me the right way, he asked my grandma to watch after me. He moved into a house in the suburbs when he made it big. He kept our small house near Grandma's house, and since he didn't sell it and it was still ours, he wanted me to live there and help take care of my grandparents. 'Who would take care of me?' was the question. I was still little at the time! I only lived in the small house because he didn't trust me to be alone in his big house when he was away. The only time I got to live in the big house was when he came home. So, in a way, the little house was my own home. The small space contained so many painful memories, but at least I was close to my grandparents' home. My grandma protested. Dad was practically giving me away to her. He was smart though. He told the courts that it was just temporary. The judge said that if he could keep both houses up and running and support me financially, on his own, he could have custody. Pretty confusing, huh?

Thank God for my grandma. She has always been my best friend. I was so glad to have her in my life! She was so wise and understanding about my weaknesses in school. She was always glad to help me, and if I could, I'd live with her permanently.

I opened the screen door.

"I have the mail," I told her. I sat down and bit into an apple.

"After I read this, we'll make dinner. How about chicken fajitas tonight?"

"Sure!" I smiled. She knew that fajitas were my favorite kind of food.

"After I read this, go to your house and get a few things for the week. When you come back, get that homework done!"

Grandma Benny tore the envelope and sighed.

"It's from your mother."

"I knew it," I said. Grandma Benny started reading.

"Dear Mom and Amber, It has been a while since we talked, but I won't be here forever. My boyfriend, Jida Jr-"

"Wasn't he arrested for the possession of drugs three times?"

"I don't know! Anyway, Jida bailed me out with his mom, Shaniqua's money."

"Woooow," we both said.

"I hope she doesn't come back with those fools!"

"Amber! You are not using your Christian spirit. We must welcome her back with open arms."

"Whatever."

Grandma scowled at me before continuing. "We went out to celebrate at Chick-Fil-A."

"MC Hammer could do better." I chuckled.

Grandma Benny tried to keep a serious face to save herself from laughing.

"And…. she spelled celebrate wrong."

"Wow!"

"It says she is coming here one of these days to see us."

"She better not." I snapped. "I don't want to see that evil b-…"

"Amber, I know what you were going to say. Enough," she said sharply.

"Sorry."

"Amber, I know your feelings about your mom, but you should at least *try* to forgive her. That's what the Bible says!"

"Did she *try* to stick to the rehab program, or did she escape twice?"

"Hush up now, girl!"

"Sorry again," I mumbled.

"Forget this ever happened, and let's make dinner. But, don't forget to do your home work. You know that the Harvard kids don't forget."

"Come on, Grandma. You know that I'm not smart enough to get into Harvard or any college for that matter!"

"It has nothing to do with your grades, but it does have something to do with your attitude. Remember, you can do *all* things through Christ who strengthens you!"

"Ok, you're right. Can you help me with my geometry and chemistry tonight? I brought my textbooks; I know how you like to teach from them. Can Grandpa help me with my American history assignment?"

"He sure can. You know your smarty pants grandpa." She bent down and kissed my forehead. "Get the chicken and peppers out."

Grandma turned her old radio on and started dancing to Gloria Gaynor's *I Will Survive*.

She took a pot, and put it on the stove.

After cleaning and seasoning the chicken breasts, she dropped them into the pot. I added the green, red, and orange peppers. She added chicken stock and let it sit to cook. Later, we took out the condiments, folded the chicken into a wrap, and sat down to eat.

"Bam!" Grandma said while presenting me with a party bag and a big box.

I tore off the wrapping paper to find the easel that I had wanted since I saw it in an art catalog last month. It was a professional easel that cost a lot of money. Christmas was about five months away and my birthday was four months away! Man, I loved my grandma. I opened the bag to find a new set of pastels and a new set of paints.

"Thanks, Grandma. Why did you do this for me?"

"Well, we happened to be dropping by an art store when I saw that lovely easel that you had wanted. Grandpa told me about how your gold pastels and paints were very old, so we bought you new ones! Do you like them?"

"Yes" I said. I gave her a big hug.

"Your grandpa and I hope that you would come with us to the art museum on Saturday, too! The show starts right after our eleven o'clock class." She grinned. "So, how do you like your presents?"

"I don't like them…"

"Well why not…?"

"I *love* them!"

She slapped my arm playfully. She knew me so well!

* * *

After dinner, I walked to my house two blocks away. I walked in, turned off the alarm, and ran upstairs to pack a few outfits. I grabbed my hairbrush and my toothbrush, and then I set the house alarm again. I was just about to leave when the phone rang.

"Man!" I walked back in and turned off the alarm. "Hello"

"Amber, It's Claudia. Do you want to go to the beach this Saturday with me, Kyla, Mike, Paige, and *Brad*?" She sang out Brad's name. She was so open about her crush on him that everyone in America probably knew about it.

"I would love to," I said.

"Grea---"

"But this Saturday I'm going with my family to an art museum."

"Oh! Your mom's back from jail?"

I cringed. "No, she's not back." I paused.

"Who are you going with then?"

"Actually, I'm going with my grandparents. There's this new Cleopatra exhibit that--" I said, getting excited.

"And miss out on seeing Brad? I'll pass, besides last time I checked, grandparents weren't exactly the *cool* type. I mean your grandpa collects small, plastic battleships, for crying out loud. Ew! OMG, so I heard Brad's grandparents are throwing a pool party for him and all of his friends, during spring break. I mean, how cool is that?"

"Whatever!" I slammed down the phone. She was my best friend, but sometimes she could get really mean. She was supposed to understand my relationship with my grandparents. She knew that it was the only real family I had left. She could act as uppity as she wanted, because I had something she could never have. I had real love at my grandparents' house always waiting for me. I smiled at that thought and set the alarm.

I went outside and smelled the fresh air and reflected about my grandparents. Nothing could tear me away from them. I spent so much time with them that I knew every Earth, Wind, and Fire song by heart. I made a decision. From here on in, if anybody asked me who my parents were, I would tell them all about my beautiful grandparents.

* * *

"So, that means that 14 times pi equals the quantity of nine times the variable 'x' minus pi?" I said enthusiastically

"Ding, ding, ding!" my grandma said. "You are correct!"

"Thanks, Grandma. Hopefully I'm ready for the math test tomorrow."

"You're welcome, Honey," she said. "Okay, study some more. I'll be waiting for your grandpa to come home. I'll be downstairs, if you need me."

"But, Grandma, isn't 'Keep It Up' on tonight?" I whined.

"Sure it is! But if you want to ace that math test of yours, you will need to 'keep it up' with more studying. I'll give you a choice. You can either study or... study! It's your choice."

"Okay," I grumbled. I gave up and started studying geometry theorems. When Grandma said something, she stuck to it. I studied hard because this was the last test before progress reports went out. I wanted a B so badly.

* * *

After studying geometry terms for an hour, I sat down and flipped through an old scrapbook. I saw a picture of my mom and me eating ice cream out on the front porch. I remembered how she put the ice cream on her finger and smeared it on my nose, just as the camera flashed. I looked so shocked from the cold feeling. My mom was laughing. Those were the good days! I turned the page to find a portrait of my mom, dad, and me standing by a Christmas tree. I wish I could go back to that very moment, where we were all one happy family. Things were always better when we did everything together. I remember walks on the beach and going out to eat on Father's Day. Who knows how things could have gone from great to damaging?

* * *

As I stepped off the bus the next day with Claudia, I stopped and stared at my grandma's house. There was a beat up pickup truck in my grandma's driveway. Hopefully, it was my Uncle Michael who was home from studying art in Spain. He was one of the most accomplished men in my family. Anything was better than living in such a poor neighborhood. He always had the best stories. I was really excited that he decided to show up in the nick of time. Now I could show them both my A+ on my math test. "Guess what else Brad did?" Claudia asked with enthusiasm.

"Claudia, I have to go," I told her while focusing on the car. "I'll call you later?"

"Um…uh… sure?"

I ran three small houses down and turned the corner. I flew through the door.

"Guess what, Uncle Mike?" I said, closing the door behind me. Instead of finding Uncle Mike, I found my mother… and my grandma laughing… and talking.

"Amber, hey!" A medium sized woman wearing a baseball t-shirt and torn jeans rushed over to me with open arms, expecting a hug. Her fingertips brushed my bare arm, sending a chill through my spine.

"DON'T TOUCH ME!" I exploded and slapped her hand away.

"Amber, didn't you get my letter?"

"Grandma, how could you do this to me?"

"Amber, come into the kitchen for a second." She took my hand. "I'll be right back," she told my mother. Grandma led me to the kitchen.

"Grandma, why?" I started to cry.

"I thought that you two could use a talk. I was trying to help you both. I want what's best for you and your mother, and that is to talk it out! I want you to solve your problems! I want---"

"Well, what about what *I* want?" I screamed. "You know how I feel about that skank! Why didn't you warn me? I trusted you! You know that, you old piece of junk. I hate you so much! Are you crazy or something? Go away. I never want to see you for as long as I live!" I stood up and gathered my things, running for the door.

"Amber…Honey…come and sit down." My mother put her hand on my shoulder and I shrugged it off. "Amber? Why are you acting this way?"

"Shut up, you…you dog! You are *not* my mother. You are a disgrace to this family. You are an embarrassment. How dare you come back after all these years!" I yelled in her face. I found a nearby portrait of our family and smashed it to the ground. The glass shattered. Grandma started to cry. "Just to let you know, I got an A+ on my math test! I would say thank you, but I can't. I won't. You don't deserve anything, especially a 'thank you'. I HATE YOU!" I spat. I could see the never-ending tears stream down her face, but I didn't care. I ran out of the door, slammed it shut, and ran all the way home.

* * *

When I got home, I couldn't stop pacing around the room. I trusted the old hag with my feelings. How could she do this to me? She knew how I felt more than anyone else. If she was being so friendly to her now, who knows how much she could've been talking to her before I found out? That thought left a terrible taste in my mouth.

I decided to take a hot shower to calm down. I was hoping that when I got out of the shower, time would rewind like it all never happened. I was in the middle of rinsing my hair when the phone rang. Come on! I turned off the shower and dried off. This had better be important.

"Hello."

"Amber, listen. I know you hate me." I grew numb at the sound of that familiar voice.

"Of cour…"

"Listen, your grandma just lost control and had a heart attack. I'm at the hospital. Get here, quickly! She doesn't look well." I hung up and sprinted to my room. I threw some clothes on, and used a towel to quickly dry my hair. I bolted to my closet and put my flip flops on. My hair was so messed up and my clothes were so wrinkled. I didn't care what I looked like. My grandma needed me. I found my bike on the side of the house and peddled as fast as I could. I peddled up to the hospital and locked my bike. People gave me strange looks as I sprinted to the front desk.

"Benvelia Marone!" I quickly said.

"Are you okay?" the receptionist at the desk asked suspiciously.

"I'm fine!" I barked. "Benvelia Marone."

"Room 3309." I ran past the elevator and to the steps. I needed to get there immediately! I looked around trying to find the right direction. The hospital smell made me nauseous. I finally found my way and ended up in the 330 hallway. "Oh my gosh!" I said when I opened the door and saw Grandma Benny. She looked like a tiny creature covered in a big blanket. I gasped at the tiny figure. She was hooked up to many tubes and wore a mask was over her face.

I rushed beside her and held her hand. The screen that showed her breathing patterns had a line that was moving up and down, but it kept flowing partly flat. Grandpa was in the corner crying into my mom's shoulder. If I wasn't so mad I would've marched up to her and told her what I thought of her. But I knew that if my grandma could hear me, she wouldn't approve.

I was so worried! If I hadn't stormed out and left her in tears she wouldn't have went crazy. She wouldn't have had a heart attack. It was my fault. Being so close with her, I knew every ailment that she had, from osteoporosis to diabetes. I sat with her at every doctor appointment and held her hand when she had to get her blood drawn frequently. I was there with her when the doctor said she had high blood pressure and needed to stay away from stressful situations. I was even there when she had a low blood sugar scare two years ago. I could quote every medication she needed by heart. I had done more research about diseases than a scientist! I knew all of this and yet I still said what I did. I am so selfish! I can't even believe what I have done.

A nurse who was already in the room held up grandma's wrist to check her pulse. The nurse paused for a few seconds and rushed to a machine. She did a double take at grandma's bed. Then she took her Walkie-talkie and yelled, "Code red! Code red! Come quick!" Six doctors rushed in, checked the machine, and felt her pulse.

"Young lady," a man barked, "You need to go now! Quick! Hurry!" He quickly ushered my mom and grandpa out of the room.

"I'm not going! You can't tell me when to leave," I said.

The doctor rolled his eyes and pulled my arm. He dragged me to the door. I stretched to find something to hold on to.

"Grandma! I love you! I'm so sorry! I love you! I love you!" That's all I got in before the door was slammed in my face. I slid down the wall and pounded on the door.

"Grandma! Don't leave me! Don't leave! I love you! I love you!" I shrieked. Someone gave me a big hug. I turned around. It was my mom. I didn't have anyone else to comfort me, so I just sat and cried. She gave me a big reassuring squeeze. It felt like the time that I fell off of my bike and broke my wrist. My mom rushed to me and hugged me. As much as I hated to admit it, it felt good.

* * *

Two weeks of grieving, crying, and sadness later, I found my dad, finally home, in the family room reading.

"Hi, Amber! Surprise!"

"Dad, Grandma died!" I rushed to him and hugged him.

"I know, Sweetie, I know."

"You know? So why didn't you come back early for the funeral?"

"Eddie, Honey, did you tell Amber yet?" A pretty little woman came into the room and sat on the couch. Her diamond studs shone through her dark silky hair. She put her feet on the table and started flipping through TV channels.

"Who is she? What is she talking about?"

"Veronica, Darling, I thought I asked you to wait upstairs," he whispered.

"Who is she? What is she talking about?" I asked again, raising my voice.

"Ed, I told you this was a bad idea!" Veronica frowned.

"Amber, we are engaged." The girl smiled and showed her ring.

"You're what? So you come back from Europe, engaged? You know that Grandma is dead? Did you know that outside your double life you have a daughter at home? You must be on something if you can't see you chose that thing." I pointed in her face. "Over your dead in-law! I can't talk to you right now! She's dead, you idiot! How could you?" I ran upstairs. What was he thinking? I lost my grandma and my dad in the same month.

* * *

I spent two months just trying to deal with life's changes. Grandma was gone, and so was my dad. He had turned into some sort of alien, always with that Veronica girl. I tried to avoid trouble, so I didn't bring up the fact that I hated that Veronica robot woman. I don't know what my dad was thinking! She wasn't pretty up close. She wore way too much makeup, and she was secretly anorexic. When I tried to tell my dad that she refused to eat, he laughed in my face. And if that wasn't crazy enough, he made an excuse for her when one of his bank accounts ended up with nothing left inside. The big house felt even emptier now that we were all living in it. Things were bad all over. I needed a sign that things would change for the better.

I prayed a lot, and I read the Bible. I even attended Grandma's old church after her funeral. I spent my time with my grandpa while Veronica and my dad partied in Vegas. Talk about selfish. It was hard to believe in God when everything was all chaos. I couldn't live this life. There had to be some other way!

* * *

One morning, after my father had finally returned, I woke up in a fog. I looked up at my alarm clock. It was 10:06 am. I put my head back down on my tear soaked pillow. It was 10:06! I was missing school! I stormed out of bed and ran to my dad's room. I found a note. It read,

Amber,
I know that you have been really stressed out, so Veronica
and I agreed that you should stay home today. We are at
Veronica's mother's spa for massages. I really need it! There's
some food downstairs. Relax!

Love,
Dad and Veronica.

Gee, I wonder why I need relaxation! I crumpled up the letter and flopped on his bed. "Dad," I said to the paper. "You're never there for me. You never were!"

My phone rang.

"Hello," I answered.

"Oh, Amber, I know you've had it rough with your grandparents, but I really need to borrow your English notes from last week, when I wasn't here. I went to Costa Rica with Brad's family."

"Um…"

"Thanks! I'm sending our vacation pics to your phone as we speak! You are going to love the one that we took at the beach."

"My grandma died, you idiot!" I barked. "And you can't talk about anything else except for Brad?" No one said anything for a moment.

"Lately, you haven't been with us. And we feel betrayed!"

"We? Who's we?"

"Amber, darling! You're holding us back!"

" Well, maybe it's because I'm having a really tough time, and you don't care, you backstabber. You are so self-centered!"

"Shut up! Such a worry freak, gosh. Stop talking. You don't make any sense. Stop crying for your grandma and wake up!"

"You need to wake up."

I pressed END on my phone until my finger started to hurt.

Remember what I had felt earlier? Now one thing was clear… I lost my grandma, my father, and my friends.

* * *

"Grandpa! I'm here! Where's Grandma?"

"What?" Grandpa asked, as I came into their house.

"That is a stupid, stupid question."

"Oh, no! I am so sorry. I'm so stupid. How could I forget?" I hit my head.

"You're not stupid. You just forget sometimes. I do too. I woke up this morning and went downstairs thinking that she would be there making tea and humming to the birds." He gave me a tight hug. "Would you like some tea?" he asked. "I'll make Benvelia's favorite." He sighed. "Mmmm, chamomile…" Grandpa remembered.

He walked over to the stove and put Grandma's favorite kettle over the fire.

"She was really something," he said, scratching his small gray beard. "I remember one night, I woke up and found my lady writing your mother letters and making a care package that she swore she would send to her in jail. She filled that package with your mother's favorites. Hmmm. Jiffy peanut butter, vanilla wafers, and even chocolate covered strawberries! Benvelia was a giver – man was she a giver. I love that lady more than I do myself." He started to cry. "I just can't live without her."

He grabbed my hand and squeezed it tight. "God's lucky….. He can see her every day in heaven…"

I stood up and gave him a strong hug. He was making me cry.

"I did it!" I confessed. "I killed her. All she wanted was for me to be happy and what do I do? I killed her…" I felt faint. I couldn't stand up any longer. Suddenly, I was on the floor and Grandpa was right there rubbing my head. He helped me stand up and led me to the nearby chair.

"Listen to me, Amber. You did not kill her, so stop saying it. You are only human. *I* am only human….. Now your grandmother was never a selfish woman. She never asked for much, but she wished that someday you'd go to a great college. You see, there is a difference between wanting something and wishing and praying that it will happen," he scolded. "Night after night she would pray for you. She wished that you would see your full potential. She never asked for much, but she wanted you to live your life up to the pinnacle of your potential."

I was starting to feel better. It was not my fault that God had chosen that moment for my grandma to join Him in heaven.

"She wanted you to go to college. Do it for your grandmother…. Do it for Benvelia."

Dear Grandpa,

College is amazing! You were right, Princeton is a great school. I'm doing really well in class. There are so many opportunities for me here. My roommate's name is Monica and she reminds me a lot of Grandma. She makes the same cookies that Grandma used to make. She likes to knit like Grandma. It's nice to have a taste of Grandma through Monica. I'm taking art classes on the weekends, like you told me. I painted a portrait of you and me, and you will love it! Dad and Veronica said that when I get back in a month, they are taking me to the Poconos for Christmas. They said that I can bring 2 people. I chose you...and Grandma. I miss you a lot. Please send some more of Grandma's fudge brownies-they're sooooo delicious. I love you! Write back soon. I can't wait to see you on Christmas.

You were right. I am only human.
I'll see you soon!

Love,
Amber

I Am Human: *Fear thou not; for I am with thee: be not dismayed; for I am thy God: I will strengthen thee; yea, I will help thee; yea, I will uphold thee with the right hand of my righteousness.*

- ISAIAH 41:10

I Am Smart

"That's right, Chris!" Mr. Sommers said for like the twentieth time today. "This class is why I teach!" He slid his glasses up his nose. "I teach to inspppire!" He spit when he pronounced the 'p's'. "I teach to lift up the heads of our future senators and neurologists. The first man to walk on Pluto will come from my class, if I have my way, and by following the direction of our very own Chris Turchin, this will all be possible."

"Any questions?" asked Chris.

This was finally my chance to impress Mr. Sommers.

"Chris."

"Yes," my stepbrother said, sighing.

"You focused on the fact that Uranus is larger than Neptune because of its diameter, so doesn't that mean that Uranus has larger mass?"

"Very good question, Claire!" I smiled. "But really you are all around wrong!" My smile faded. "You see, size has nothing to do with mass! You would be foolish to assume so, although to get a diameter you must first have the circumference," he said. "This surely is a another matter that I am sure you'd be better off discussing with Mrs. Manors who would be full of gusto to teach you about circumference!" Everyone knew Mrs. Manors was the meanest teacher in all of Charles Kertan High School!

"Yes, maybe," Mr. Sommers said. "Good idea, Chris. I'll call her right now!" While my mouth hung open, and Mr. Sommers called, Chris walked up to my desk and whispered, "You really shouldn't let your mouth hang open. You might attract flies!" I closed my mouth quickly. "And by the way, Uranus has smaller mass than Neptune, Einstein!" He punched my temple in slow motion.

"Claire, it's all set up!" said Mr. Sommers. "Mrs. Manors is expecting you at lunch!"

Everyone in the classroom cracked up as Jennifer Fob and Constance Spade high-fived. Chris returned to the front of the room, took a bow, took his tri-fold off the presentation desk, and returned to his seat. As he walked, Constance, the most popular girl in school, winked at him! I couldn't even get a member of the Glee Club to nod at me! How did he do it? For him, it came naturally, because when you come from a genius family, that's what happens. There is, however, one exception to the forever genius clan, which is their downfall. Guess what it is! I can tell you, it is me.

The bell rang and everyone but Constance, who was obliviously reapplying lip gloss, left.

"Ms. Evens. May I have a word with you?" Mr. Sommers asked. I walked to his desk and he wasted no time grilling me like a meat patty.

"Ms. Evens, the other teachers and I have discussed that your grades have gone from A's in the ninth grade to now D's in my class and in others in your sophomore year. What's the deal?"

"Well," I started.

"Claire," he interrupted, "I spoke with the principal, and since you're almost failing, I referred you to the school's scholastic team to make up for your incomplete credits."

"What? Are you trying to kill me?" I asked.

"Um, no. I am just trying to ensure you a decent GPA! I would like to see you pass the tenth grade."

Oh, Lord! What would my parents say? 'You destroyed the Evens-Turchin family once and for all!' or maybe 'Claire, I don't know what you were thinking. Let's make her take the stupid test that our neighbor's cat took last month!'

"Actually, Mr.Turchin…Cameron …"

"Huh?" I wouldn't let him finish his thought. Cameron was not in charge of me, even if he was 21!

"Your stepbrother!"

"I know!" I snapped.

In the background, Constance giggled. I wanted to smack that MAC blush right off her face!

"Bye, Mr. S!" she purred and walked out of the classroom.

"Ms. Evens, the choice has been made. I will send the information to your mother. Please hurry along now. I have a class in three minutes."

"What?" I squeaked. "I don't get a pass?"

"I don't give passes, Ms. Evens. You know that."

I was expecting him to say *'Dumb girls with no future don't deserve passes!'*

I walked out of the classroom, silent tears and all, past the office, through the corridor, and out the breezeway door. It was raining.

* * *

Three periods later, I was sitting in Spanish class, bored to tears. Thank God it was the last ten minutes of class. I had to go to the bathroom so badly! Once we were dismissed, I burst through the wooden door of C-15 and bolted. The amazing Olympic track star, Alyson Felix, would have been proud or my fast sprint!

I walked into the bathroom and noticed a familiar Vera Wang makeup bag on the counter before I went into the opened stall. Then I heard some girls talking. I knew who they were because I could spot their matching pink Tom's from anywhere!

"And she's like a stupid wannabe!" Fiona said.

"Like when I found out she was related to Chris Turchin, and I said like 'Shut the front door!' They can't be related! She's like a total spaz, and like he's like a major like smart guy!" Jennifer added, sounding even dumber than ever.

They were talking about me! I froze in my position in the stall.

"Not to mention Chris is totally cute! He's a full package!" Constance said.

I imagined Chris as literally a full package on its way to Antarctica.

"I know one thing, though---".

"Fiona! Did you just drop my new liquid eyeliner? What's wrong with you?!" Jennifer yelled.

"Jen, shush! Like I was saying," Talisha said, "my sister, Grace, knows Claire's sister, Cassy, and she says that everyone in her family is smart! Gosh, she's such a liar! Dumbbell is stupid, and she's a part of their family."

"You just gave me the perfect idea. Jen, pass me my new creamsicle gloss! Anyway, Dumbbell has a new nickname. It's

…… Taco Bell!" The girls burst with laughter. "Because serving tacos is the closest thing she'll ever get to success!" Fiona giggled.

"I bet Taco Bell already has a uniform with her name on it," Constance added.

"Oh my God! My mom just bought these new aprons for our chefs and like…"

Their voices faded as they left the bathroom. I started to cry, wishing I could just melt and be flushed out to sea like everybody wanted. I imagined the ride down the pipes would be more peaceful.

* * *

The remainder of the day was blurry. The teachers spoke, but I ignored them. Instead, I doodled in my notebooks. They asked questions, and I answered, "I don't know." I wish they'd just back off. Things were already said. I knew that everybody hated me, so what was the point of responding to the world? Normally, I'd look forward to going home, but I realized that home was no sunny day with rainbows either. Cameron ratted me out, and Chris made me feel even more stupid. The only ones left were Cassy and Caylie, but by now "Cursing Claire Fever" had most likely claimed them, too. Walking to class, I passed by Constance, who winked at me as if she knew my secrets. Just then, I understood why.

Bobby Maris walked up to me, and do you know what he said to my face? He said, "How would you like your taco, sir? With chicken or cheese?" He high-fived Constance as I stood by and said nothing.

Bobby may as well have slapped me square in the face.

"What's wrong, Claire?" Caylie asked. "You don't like my chicken pot pie?"

"I love it, Cay. I'm just not hungry." I pushed my food around my plate when finally it occurred to Caylie, my 22 year-old sister, that something was wrong.

"I'll tell you!" Chris yelled, his eyes glued to the TV. "Ohhh! Did you see that pass? Reggie's on fire!"

"Yeeeeah, man!" Cameron agreed. They clinked glasses of iced tea.

"Why won't you both just sit at the table like regular human beings?" Cassy, my 17 year- old sister asked.

"Shut up, Cass!" Cameron yelled. "Ohhhhhh!"

"You guys didn't even say anything about this dinner that I slaved over." Caylie announced.

"It's goo…. Scoooore!" Chris yelled.

"Cam, did you get your schedule for your next semester at Yale?" Cassy asked.

"None of your business," Cam said, still focused on the game. He stuck his feet on the coffee table. Cassy got up, rolled up a newspaper and whacked his legs.

"Owww! What was that for?" Cassy stormed back to the table and rolled her eyes.

"Cay, let me know when your next break from Harvard starts. I need to tell Cammy so she can plan our vacation in Punta Cana," Cameron muttered while chewing his chicken.

"Mom said that in order to go, she needs to find out about Cassy's acceptance into Cornell," Caylie said. "The mail won't be touched here when we are in Punta Cana."

I drank my iced tea absent mindedly.

"That's so dumb!" Chris yelled. "Everyone knows Cassy's not going to Cornell because Stanford gave her a full ride."

"I know. Mom wants me to weigh out my options!"

"I know," Cameron said. "All I'm saying is that if Stanford gave me a full scholarship for volleyball, I'd go there!"

"Thanks for the wisdom, Buddha!" Cassy snorted.

"I don't see why you have to go next year, anyway. You are only 17 and skipped a grade. It's not like you're 18 like every other senior. Why couldn't you just wait like everyone else?" Cam asked.

"Why couldn't you have a smaller head like everyone else?" Cassy challenged.

Meet my modern family of Einsteins!

"When's Cammy coming home?" Chris said with a burp. I rolled my eyes. He was finally paying attention to us because it was halftime.

"Mom said she'll be home in an hour," Caylie announced. "And she expects homework to be done, Claire and Chris!"

"Can you help me with my math homework?" I asked Cassy.

"She's getting all the help she can get", Chris mumbled, but still loud enough for everyone to hear. "She's seeing Mrs. Manors at lunch every day for some special attention!" "Crap! No Evens-Turchin has ever needed extra help before. Now baby Turchin's rep is totally trashed!" Cassy smiled at her own joke, but I did not think it was funny at all.

"Cammy and Dad's baby'll be fine," Cameron assured her.

"Poor Mom and Greg," Cassy sighed.

Great! Now I was a disgrace!

"Way to just say it all in my face, guys!" I yelled jumping up.

"We'd say it behind your back, but then you wouldn't hear it." Chris said, his expression serious.

"Shut up!" Cassy commanded, whacking Chris with the same folded newspaper.

"Owww!" I heard Chris shout.

I ran upstairs and slammed my door. Caylie ran after me.

"I hate my stupid life!" I shouted, and threw my pillows at the wall. I collapsed on my bed and, somehow, I fell asleep.

* * *

I woke up to the ringing phone. I needed to talk to my mom. I picked up the receiver in my room, prepared to say hi, when I heard Cassy talking.

"Hey, Cass!" my mom started. She sounded very tired.

"Hi, Mom! How's Baby Turchin?"

"She's fine, always kicking."

"You're a fool for staying at work so long. You're practically nine months pregnant, for goodness sake."

"I know. I know! Don't start with me!" Mom took a deep breath just how she practiced with the doctor. "I called to say that my flight was cancelled due to rain, so I'll be home in the morning."

"How are you getting along?

"Fine. I just had something from the Salad Works at the airport, so I'm fine."

"Don't forget! You are eating for two!" Cassy sang in a high pitched voice.

"Yeah."

I was this close to sneezing, but I looked up, put my finger to the bottom of my nose and whispered "pineapple!"

"Cassy, did you just say 'pineapple'?" Mom asked.

Snap!

"Nope!"

"I must be hearing things," Mom noted. "How are your brothers and sisters?"

"Everyone's fine except for Claire." I almost shrieked. WHAT?!

"Well, what's wrong?"

"Ever since Cam signed her up for that scholastic team, she's been freaking out."

Thanks a lot Cassy!

"I don't know about this scholastic team," Mom said. "Claire's very shy."

"Personally, I think that Claire needs it. She'll make new friends and she can work on her all around skills."

"You know how hard your sister works."

"I do, but I don't think it's enough."

"Maybe she needs a tutor," Mom suggested.

"Maybe."

"I mean, with the new money that Greg is making, we could afford a really professional tutor."

"I think that's a great idea! And Greg's totally the best new stepfather ever, by the way." She was only saying that because Greg let her go to the Paramore concert last Thursday night, a school night.

"Good! I'm glad you think so. I'll talk to Greg about it. Give me someone else." "CHRIS!" Cassy shrieked. "MOM'S ON THE PHONE!!"

"Coming!" I heard Chris call.

"Bye, Mommy! Take care of Baby Turchin!" Cassy made kissing sounds into the phone, and I hung up, too sad to listen to Chris talk.

Several minutes later, Caylie and Cassy knocked on my door. Claire, can we come in?" Caylie asked.

I tried to hold back my anger before saying, "Yeah, sure! One minute."

I grabbed a tissue and wiped my face, threw it out, and opened the door.

"Have you been crying?" Cassy asked.

"No," I said quickly.

Caylie sat on the edge of the bed.. "We know things have been pretty weird around here, but…"

"Chris hates me. What have I done to him?" I exploded into tears. "I know I'm dumb. You don't need to say anything because you know it's true!"

"Claire!" Cassy hugged me. "That is not true." I wondered if I should tell her that I knew what she said to mom. "You are so not dumb. You're smart. Not everyone was blessed with school smarts."

"Tell that to the God who made this family all smart except for me!" I shouted. "Claire," Caylie started, "not everyone is book smart, but you are smart about other things!"

"Like what?"

"Like….common sense smart and life skills smart!"

"I don't have common sense," Cassy offered.

"I know!" I glared at her.

"Claire, what did I do?" Cassy asked innocently. She tried to rub my back.

"Don't touch me!" I screamed. "How could you not hear me when you were ratting me out to Mom?"

"What?" Cassy asked.

"Don't act like you don't know what I'm saying. I'll need a tutor, remember?"

"What's going on?" Caylie said.

"Ask the traitor," I mumbled. "Cassandra Amy Evens- Turchin and Caylie Heather Evens- Turchin, I can't do this. Get out of my room, now!" I said in one big blurt.

Cassy timidly walked out and Caylie looked confused, but I didn't care. I needed to stop thinking about what they wanted for me and more about what I wanted for myself. I needed to stop everything. Stop attempting. Stop wishing. Stop dreaming. Stop trying. Yeah, that's it. Stop trying!

* * *

"Let's review what's on your Chapter 6 quiz," Ms. O'Brian said. "Okay! It's on vocab, the Vietnam War, the veterans of the war, and all of your notes."

The class sighed. "Am I talking to a brick wall here, people?" she asked with her hands on her hips. The only reason that many people weren't asleep in this class was because Ms. O'Brian was young and pretty.

"Okay, class, let's watch a video about those Vietnam War heroes." She leaned in towards me and another dumb kid and said, "If I were you guys, I'd take notes." I knew that she was trying to help me, but I felt very embarrassed. She walked to the Smart Board and hit play. As usual, the lights dimmed and most of the kids instantly closed their eyes. I personally was too busy writing a letter to free me from the scholastic team to care about Ms. O'Brian and her side notes! Finally, I settled on this wording.

Dear Mr. Girgisan,
My daughter, Claire Evens-Turchin, will not be able to
attend the scholastic meets and practices because of a recent
death in the family. The funeral is coming up soon and we'll
be leaving for Denver today. I'm sorry, but she will also be
missing the regional competition, but I'll keep you posted. If
you have any questions, please contact me at (702) 555-0126.

Thanks.
Camille Evens-Turchin

I quickly compared the signature to my report card slip's signature and smiled. No one needed to know that that number was my cell phone number! This would get me off the hook until after the regional competition.

After class, I went to the office and dropped off the note to be sent to Mr. Girgisan. Everything was going to be all right! The bell rang and I went to Mr. Sommers's class for science.

On my way in, Mr. Sommers stopped me.

"How's scholastic practice going?" he asked.

"It's swell!" I lied. "I'm really learning a lot ."

"That's great for you," Mr. Sommers said.

"Thanks," I mumbled, walking to my seat.

"Okay class, attention! Class give a warm welcome to Ms. Torid," A brunette woman with choppy bangs and rosy cheeks waved to us from behind the chemistry desk. We all clapped.

"You know that Ms. Torid has been student teaching for this class, and today she will be teaching you all on her own."

"Can I go and grab a coffee?" I heard Mr. Sommers ask.

"Yeah, sure. Go ahead," she replied enthusiastically.

"Class, behave!" he commanded, using a warning deep tone.

"So I see that you all have been finishing your extra credit presentations," she said, looking at her plans. "Today we will be continuing Chapter 21, section 1. Let's warm up with a worksheet,." she said, passing them out .

"Okay, class. Times up!" Ms. Torid announced. "Let's go around the room. Sabrina. Number one."

"Mitosis," Sabrina answered.

"Yes." Ms. Torid smiled, and so did Suck-Up-Sabrina.

"Number two. Um…..Khristian," she said, looking at the seating chart.

"Anaphase."

"Yes. Number three. Anastasia."

"Telophase."

"Yes. Number four. Chris."

"Prophase, Ms. Torid," Chris said, grinning as if he were smiling for tooth paste ad.

"Yes. Number five, Michael."

"Metaphase," he said, messing with his contacts.

"Correct. Number six. Claire."

"Don't know, don't care," I replied.

"Ohhhhh!" everyone started whispering.

"Nice one, Claire!" Constance purred, looking shocked.

"Um…," Ms. Torid, said flustered. "Um….let's move on." She giggled nervously.

"Number six. Taylor."

Chris turned around and looked at me as if I just told him that I would be murdering him tonight at midnight!

"What?" I mouthed. He rolled his eyes. I had nothing to lose. It was working.

* * *

"I'm telling Mom!" Chris said on the bus.

"What?"

"You heard me!" he challenged.

"Chris, I have nothing to lose. You need to stop worrying before you get grey hair. If I'm not smart, I need to face it and move on."

"I'm still telling," he said. "You're even more stupid for not trying!"

"If you tell her, I swear you'll be dead." Knowing very well that I could fight him, Chris was instantly silent. This is the last he spoke of it for a month.

* * *

Life is good. Who would have thought that I would get by a month without trying? Sure, teachers called home asking about my behavior, but I deleted every message before Mom had the chance to listen to it. Maybe I was doing the right thing. Mom couldn't be stressed because she was getting ready for her baby!

I was glad that Mr. Girgisan wasn't nosy. He tried to call, but since no one answered, he gave up. Regionals were over, and I was due back already, but I had to admit this. It takes time to think of good excuses! All of my efforts came to a collapse when one day Mr. Girgisan called my mom's cell phone instead.

When I came downstairs to grab a snack, Mom was on her phone while stirring chili. I noticed that she was pretty upset.

198

By the time she exploded, 'WHAT?' I knew it was about me. I grabbed my string cheese and almost escaped up the stairs when she mouthed that she had to talk to me. She hung up; I was in for it!

"Caylie!" she yelled. "Come and stir this chili!"

"Coming, Mom," Caylie called.

"We need to talk," she said, pointing me towards the stairs "Sit," she commanded when we reached her room. Greg was lying on the bed talking on the phone. My mom gave him a crazy look, and he left.

"Where should we start? Perhaps that note that *I* wrote to Mr. Girgisan would make a nice opening! Or maybe I'll start with, and I quote 'Your rude and obnoxious behavior.' Who do you think you are?" she asked, pacing the perimeter of the room. "You certainly are not an Evens because we don't tolerate it! You certainly are not a Turchin, because we don't do disrespect! Who are you? Do you think that not trying will get you anywhere? Sure, lying will, but will honesty? I really trusted that when I married Greg, we'd all become a family, and there'd be no secrets."

"Mom," I said, "Chris hates me! He humiliates me in front of everybody. He makes me feel stupid. And thanks to him, I'm fully confident that I am an idiot. It's like I have Stupiditis. The rest of the family talks behind my back. I don't fit into the Evens-Turchin world, and I feel like a freak! I don't even have a home at home."

"Honey, then you come to me!" You should know that you can always come to me."

"Not when we don't communicate! Not when you're not home!" I said. "Mom, I love you, but we don't talk like we used to. Nothing is what it used to be!"

"That would all change, if you just came to me."

I started to cry.

"But if you don't do your schoolwork and don't try, what do you want me to do?"

"I'm sorry. I'll try. Just don't hate me."

"Claire Rae. I would never hate you. Ever." She gave me a tight hug, her pregnant belly pressing against me. "But Mr. Sommers did say that the only way for you to pass for the second marking period was to join that scholastic competition team."

"But---"

"But, nothing! You are going, and it's final. Honey, maybe you'll learn more than things for school!" I hated how she was always looking at the bright side, but that's what made her my mother. "You never know."

"Fine." I agreed. "Mommy, will you still love Baby Turchin, if she's not so smart like me?'

"It's not about how you start, it's how you finish. However, I do believe that my daughter's brain has been taken over by aliens if she'd ever think that I didn't love her! What kind of question is that?" She tickled my stomach. "And this baby'll be smart no matter what. Do you want to know why?"

"Yeah."

"Because you are her sister."

"Thanks, Mom," I hugged her.

"I will talk to all of them, as well. It is time for this household to be respectful."

* * *

By the time dinner started, everyone had apologized. Everyone but Chris. I smiled at him, but he gave me a cold stare.

I asked nicely if he could pass the cornbread; when our parents weren't looking, he rolled his eyes, and shook his head. I just didn't get it, until that night when he appeared in my doorway.

"Typical Claire! Worrying Cammy like a wart! She doesn't care about anyone, but herself."

"What?" I screamed.

"Let me talk! Ever since we moved here, everything has been about Claire's feelings. 'Don't say wittle Claire's not smart, because she'll cry!'" he cooed. "Whatever! Nothing is about me anymore!"

"And things are about me?" I asked. "Tell me how you really feel!"

"Clai---"

"You let me talk now, Chris. Cameron's fussing about Yale. Caylie's fussing about Harvard. Cassy's fussing about Stanford. Is it really about me Mr. Mommy-I-Got-Another-A plus plus?"

"Whatever, Claire! I'm just all around sick of you!"

"Yeah, like living with you is a basket of roses."

"Will both of you just shush!" Cassy came in wearing her green mint facial mask. "Chris, you go to your room! Claire, you get ready for bed."

"Fine." Chris said. "But this conversation isn't over, Claire!"

"Indeed!" I spat.

* * *

"Okay," Mr. Girgisan said to the group. "Finals are coming up, and by studying hard, we'll have a chance. Now, I have split you up into two groups. You will practice by going against each other. Group one, by the front bookcase, Charlie, Samantha, Devin, and Robyn. Group two, next to my desk, Mia, David, Claire, and Kevin."

When we all got to our groups for our scholastic team practice, we were given buzzers. Each time that a question was asked, either team would press the buzzer. The first one to press it would answer. If you answered it correctly, your team would get ten points unless the question was a double pointer.

"Are you ready?" Mr. Girgisan asked.

"Ready," we all called.

"Okay. For ten points…Augustus' peace brought a period of what, which lasted for 200 years?"

Charlie pressed his buzzer. "Pax Romana!" he answered confidentially.

"Yes," Mr. Girgisan said.

What?! I didn't remember who Augustus was! Maybe the next one would be easier.

"The Roman Catholic Church started a custom of not eating what on Fridays, in early times?"

Mia quickly pressed his buzzer. "Meat," she said, smiling.

"Yes. Team one has ten points. Team two has ten points. Next question."

Who knew what he was talking about, oh I forgot…smart people! I couldn't let this get me down. Perhaps I would know the next answer.

"Okay. If I said 'le cahier' meaning notebook… which language would I be speaking?"

"Easy one," David said, pressing the buzzer.. "French!"

"Yes. Good job, David."

How did he know that?

"Next. What word means the change in direction of a wave when it travels from one material to another?"

I knew this one! I buzzed in.

"Refraction!" I yelled.

"Yes, Claire! Good job." Mia gave me a high five. The others looked at me as if I had ten heads. They were shocked.

"Ok. Team one, you have 20 points. Team two, you have 30 points. Now, let's continue."

I felt so confident, now!

"In Greek mythology, Icarus was the son of who?"

Robyn buzzed in. "Chrome!" she answered.

"Sorry, no," Mr. Girgisan replied.

Mia buzzed in. "Daedalus."

"Correct! Wow, Mia! Next, what is the nuclear reactor that produces at least as much fissionable material to use as energy as it burns as energy?"

Who knew what he was talking about? Devin buzzed in.

"Breeder reactors," he responded.

"Yes! Very good, all of you1 I'm glad to see you all working together! It's now time for the final round. Please select one group member."

Team one selected Samantha and my team selected Kevin. They both walked up to the podium.

"Now," Mr. Girgisan began, "each of you will have thirty seconds to answer as many questions as possible. If they are correct, you get ten points. If they are not, you get nothing. Sam, you're up."

Sam walked up to her microphone.

"Okay. The faint, outermost region of the sun's atmosphere is called the what?"

"Corona," she said.

"Who created the Mohs Scale?"

"Henry Mohs."

"Pytheas was a astronomer of what nationality?"

"Greek."

The timer rang.

"Times up!" he announced. "Corona was right. Henry was wrong. His name was Friedrich. Greek was correct. You earned 20 points."

"Yesss!" Samantha exclaimed.

"Next up, Kevin. Time starts…now! What is the basic unit that makes up neutrons and protons?"

"Um….a….quark."

"Whose poems were not a success until after her death in 1886?"

"Emily Dickison."

"And William Blake was famous for what two major books?"

"Songs of Experience and Songs of Time."

The timer rang.

"Kevin, quark was right. Emily Dickinson was correct, but William Blake wrote *Songs of Innocence* and *Songs of Experience*. Total points earned: 20."

"Man," Kevin responded, disappointed. Personally, I'd be happy to get even one correct!

"Time's up, kids. Great work! Nice instincts. As you know, we only have one more practice, so study hard!"

We clapped and picked up our bags. I could get used to this!

* * *

It was crunch time. All night I played songs on my iHome that were inspiring. Currently, I had *We Gonna Win* and the Rocky theme song stuck in my head. It came down to today. I would prove once and for all that Claire Rae Evens-Turchin was indeed smart. I would have this moment where all eyes went on me, and I could already hear the chants from the crowd!

"Good morning, Mom!" I said coming down the stairs. Mom was in the kitchen eating watermelon covered in peanut butter, her latest craving. "Mom, you have to stop with those odd cravings!" I told her.

"Yeah, Mom! That stuff smells terrible!" Cassy walked into the kitchen and fixed her hair into a big messy bun.

"Well, good morning to you two!" Mom said offensively.

"I said good morning," I reminded her. "You just worry about your baby who is due in three days!"

"I'm trying," she said.

"How's my all-star extraordinaire?" Cameron asked, coming down the stairs. He sat on the center island. My mom stared him down until he got off. "Sorry," he mumbled. "Aren't you glad I hooked you up, Sis?" he asked me.

"Yeah, sure, whatever!" I said. "And yes, I am."

"I know I'm awesome." He laughed.

"It would be more awesome if you brushed your teeth!" Cassy noted.

"Whatever."

"Good morning!" Caylie chirped, descending the staircase in a custom T-shirt that said 'Love Me Hate Me, I'm Still Caylie!' "We gotsta hit the road in ten. Christmas sales have already started."

"Are you sure you don't want to come?" Chris asked Mom.

"What do you think, Einstein?" Cameron slapped Chris in the back of his head.

"No, I'm fine," Mom said. "I like being here with my peanut butter watermelon!"

"Gross," Cam commented.

"Okay, let's jet!" They all stood in line and took turns kissing Mom's cheek.

"Are you sure that you don't want to come?" Cassy asked me.

"I'm too nervous! I don't want to puke all over your blue tights and black boots!"

"Do what you must," she said, acting like she was gagging.

"Evens-Turchins, pile up!" Caylie yelled.

As soon as they were gone, my mom went to her room. I stayed in the kitchen studying my notes until I heard screaming coming from my mom's room. I ran to see what was wrong. Her hair was wet and her body was sweating, as if she had just run from Maine to Texas.

"Mom, what's wrong?"

"It's coming," she swallowed.

"What?"

"It's coming!" she said louder.

"What do you mean?"

"The baby!" she exploded.

OOOMMMGGG! This was not happening! Who did I call? What did I do?

I ran to the bathroom, juked myself as if I was playing football, and grabbed my cell phone from out of my pocket. I dialed Greg's cell, but there was no answer! I dialed Caylie's cell and it went right to voicemail. I dialed my grandmother's house; no one picked up!

I punched 911, but my phone battery died and it shut off. I couldn't believe this was happening!!! I tried to find one of the house phones, but I couldn't find any of them anywhere. I blamed my brothers who gathered their friends at our house to call a radio station at the same time to win concert tickets. Of course, they never put them back!

"Ahhhhh!" Mom cried out. Ahhh was right! She needed a hospital! I couldn't drive, but hey, desperate times call for desperate measures! Since the hospital was only up the street, I put my flip flops on and helped my mom to the backseat of the car.

"It's coming! It's coming!"

I turned the car on and backed out of the driveway, just how my real dad had once shown me. He was a retired NASCAR driver. I took a deep breath. I knew I could do this!

I drove down my street, made a smooth right, turned to the left and out of the development. Thank God, rush hour was over! I drove down a mile and made a right.

My mom's crying grew louder.

"I'll get you there, Mom," I said, glancing in the rearview mirror. "Almost there, Mom."

I turned left past a Wegman's and a Wal-Mart. Then I stopped at a red light, waiting for what felt like hours for it to turn green. I drove a couple more blocks, then put my turn signal on and drove into the emergency room parking lot.

I ran inside the ER. "Someone!" I called. I saw the receptionists, and ran to their desk. "My mom's in the car, and she's about to have her baby. I need help,"

"Roger! Code 1292! Code 1292!" I heard the heavyset woman call. A man whom I assumed to be Roger followed me with a gurney to the car. He and three other men lifted her up onto the stretcher and wheeled her in.

"Will she be okay?" I asked the man.

"Yes, she will. Wait here."

I went to the waiting room sweating like a pig. My adrenaline was rushing, and I ran to a nearby phone.

After the third call, Caylie finally answered .

"Hello!" She was laughing.

"Cay, Mom's having the baby!"

"What?" She stopped laughing. "What? Where is she? Hold on." She shrieked, "Evens-Turchins, mount up. Okay!" I'm back. What's going on?"

"I drove Mom to the hospital," I squeaked. My throat was suddenly bone dry.

"You what? "

"I couldn't get anyone and---"

"What hospital are you at?" she asked.

"Jefferson Memorial."

"I'll call Greg. We are fifteen away. Bye."

I hung up and sat down trying to recap what I had just done. I just broke the law. I could be arrested! I started to think about the possibilities. I imagined myself in incarcerated in jail. Just then Greg, Caylie, Cameron, Cassy, and Chris burst through the doors.

"Is she okay?" Cameron asked.

"I don't know."

"Evens-Turchin family!" a baldheaded doctor called.

"How's my Cammy?" Greg asked frantically.

"She's fine. We had a little complication because of her hyperventilating, but she's fine. She is resting now, so we'll only allow the father to see her.

Baldy led Greg down the hallway.

"Boy or Girl?" I heard Greg ask.

Caylie turned to me as did everyone else. (Talk about uncomfortable!)

"You drove?" Cassy asked in astonishment.

"Well, yeah..."

"High five!" Cassy squealed.

"What you did was irresponsible and you should---" Chris started.

"Chris, Stuff it!" Caylie warned. "I'm so proud of you!" Caylie hugged me. "And to think you thought you were dumb! That move surely wasn't dumb!"

"I guess she's all right," Chris said shyly. I smiled, and if I wasn't mistaken, Chris did too.

"Kids," Greg called. "Care to meet your knew baby sister?"

"Yeah, of course!" We all shouted in unison. We walked down the hallway and made a right into room 208.

"Ahhhh! She's gorgeous!" Caylie exclaimed.

"I know! She takes after her older sis!" Cassy said.

She had a button nose like my mom and hazel eyes like Greg's.

"Not bad, Cammy," Cameron commented.

"Thanks, son. But I think I had something to do with it, too!" Greg said playfully.

"Who volunteers to change diapers?" Mom asked in a tiny voice.

"Me!" Cassy said.

"Me!" I agreed.

"Me!" Chris said, too.

"Me!" Cameron said next.

"And me!" Caylie exclaimed.

"That's a lot of me's!" Greg said.

"So, what's her name?" I asked.

"We decided on Courtney Lynne," said Mom.

"Awwwe! Little Court Court!" Caylie cooed touching Courtney's tiny fingers.

"Ohhh, my Lord Jesus!" Cassy erupted. "Your scholastic competition started one hour ago!" We all looked at a nearby clock. Sure enough, it was 3:35.

"Okay," Caylie thought aloud. "I'll drive Claire and Cass, and you two will be picked up by Cass as soon as I get Claire settled in."

"Fine by me!" Cameron agreed as Caylie pushed me towards the door.

"Wait!" my mom cried out. The noise shocked all of us. "Come here, Claire." I walked up to her bedside. "Thanks a lot, Baby. Break a leg." I bent down and she kissed my cheek. "Now, go!" she said. "I Love you."

Cassy, Caylie, and I filed out and ran to the parking lot. When we got to the competition, Caylie walked me inside and reserved seats in the back for our family.

I walked into the cafeteria and found my team.

"Claire!" Mia ran up to me. "You're here!"

"Claire..." Mr. Girgisan said in a warning tone.

"I would have been here, but my mom had her baby and-"

"Well, there's something you don't hear every day! It's fine, but the rules state that everyone signed up must participate. We are

tied and the only round left is sudden death, which means that…
you must compete to win us our trophy."

"W-what?" I froze.

"You can do it," he said easily. "We all have faith in you!" I
remembered a scripture: I can do all things through Christ who
strengthens me; starting right now.

"I'm in," I announced.

"Yes!" Everyone cheered.

"Claire, it's time."

I walked through a door and backstage. I shivered, opening
the door as some boy on the other team made his way across the
stage and sat in one of two chairs.

"Welcome back to the finals of our Scholastic Extravaganza!" a
man announced. Both teams have 240 points, and need to break
the tie in a sudden death round!" The audience clapped. "Okay.
Kertan High School, you're up."

Oh, Lord that was me! I stepped up to the microphone.

"You have 40 seconds starting…now! In what year was
Jamestown, Virginia founded?"

"1607."

"After World War II, how many nations joined forces to
protect the world peace?"

"Fifty!" I said confidently.

"What early people developed the 365 day calendar?"

"Egyptians."

"What does the poem 'Elegy' written by Thomas Gray
discuss?"

"Ummm…." I forgot that one. I had to dig deep. Lord, please
help me. "Death!" I shouted. It had just come to me.

"Ragtime has the roots related to what type of music?"

"Five...Four...Three!" The audience counted down.

"Early Jazz!"

"Times up!" he yelled. I heard Cameron and Cassy the most. They were chanting and spelling out my full name. They were so strange.

"Sutten High School, you're up!"

The boy walked up to the same microphone.

"Time starts...now! In the early times, the words, 'slash' and 'burn' related to what?'

"Agriculture," the boy answered.

"What term describes how wide a snake can open its mouth?"

" Hinged mouths."

"As a result of the Spanish American War, what country was freed from Spanish control?

"Argentina." He smiled.

"What year did Booker T. Washington found the Tuskegee Institute?"

"Um..." He paused. ".......I ....umm...eighteen eighty...... um..."

"Five...Four...Three...Two..."

"1881!" he shouted.

"And time!" the announcer yelled. "Let's see! We'll start with Kertan High! 1607 was...correct!"

The audience clapped.

"Fifty was...correct!" Yes! "Egyptians was...correct!" All right!! "Death was...correct! And early jazz was...correct! You earned your team fifty points!!! Congratulations!"

The crowd went wild...for *me*!

The boy stood up.

"Sutten High…Agriculture was…correct! Hinged mouths was…correct! Argentina was…incorrect. I'm sorry. The answer was Cuba." The boy hung his head low.

"And…1881 was…correct. You earned your team thirty points! Congratulations!"

Each team ran on stage. "It is time for the moment of truth. Kertan High's final score is….290 points! Sutten High's final score is 270 points! That means that Kertan High School won this year's Scholastic Extravaganza! Thanks for joining us this year! We hope to see you back next year. Goodnight!"

My team rushed to my side and they all picked me up. This was too surreal. For the first time, I realized that I was smart. I had been smart from the beginning, And now it was time to shine, like God had told me all along, I would. That's it…I would shine.

Dear Diary,

Today, we are all shopping for clothes for baby Courtney. She weighs six pounds and five ounces. It's so hard to believe that she is finally here! Now, my family has two victories. Right after the competition Caylie took us all out to The Cheesecake Factory, and she let me order whatever I wanted. She told me that she knew I was smart and that if I ever doubted myself again, she would hang me upside down by my shoelaces. All along I had been smart. It took me hard work to get back to the way I once was, but it was worth the journey! Life would be pretty boring without obstacles, right? I thank God for my ability. At least I woke up this morning. My mom ensured me that from now on, the Evens-Turchin household would be a support system and, with God in our lives, I believe it is possible! I have to go now. Baby Courtney is up and it's time to play!

I Am Smart: *But of him are ye in Christ Jesus, who of God is made unto us wisdom, and righteousness, and sanctification, and redemption.*

- I Corinthians 1:30

About the author

Ashleigh Morgan, a teenager herself, she wrote "I Am" to inspire teen girls around the world, and hopes that it will have a positive impact on their lives. Each obstacle in her life has inspired her to write the stories in this book. Ashleigh believes that living your dreams and conquering life's obstacles are the best accomplishments anyone can achieve. She also believes in living life to the fullest, laughing until your face and stomach hurt, and loving until you can't love anymore!

Ashleigh lives in New Jersey with her mom, dad, and two younger brothers. She plans to study Neurology in college. In her spare time she plays volleyball, dances, loves to cook, and participates in numerous school and church activities. Ashleigh helped start the Peer Mediation club in her school to help teens solve their conflicts through verbal communication. She loves to help anyone who is in need. Ashleigh would like to thank God for everything he has done for her and everything that he will continue to do. Without Him, none of this would ever be possible.

Connect with Ashleigh at: iamashleighmorgan@gmail.com

Made in the USA
Las Vegas, NV
11 December 2020

12878767R00125